MARCO ⊕ POLO ✓

Please return on or before the last date stamped below

JS √8

WITHDRAWN - 22/07/2020

Library, Dinnington Campus
Rotherham College
Doe Quarry Lane, Dinnington, S25 2NF
Renewals/Enquiries: 01909 559279

914.14 LIE

www.marcopolouk.com

The best Insider Tips → p. 4

INSIDER TIP

Best of ... → p. 6

Sightseeing → p. 26

Food & drink → p. 50

SYMBOLS

INSIDER TIP	Insider Tip
★	Highlight
●●●●	Best of ...
☼	Scenic view
☺	Responsible travel: for eco-logical or fair trade aspects
(*)	Telephone numbers that are not toll-free

PRICE CATEGORIES HOTELS

Expensive   over 120 pounds

Moderate   75–120 pounds

Budget   under 75 pounds

The prices are for a double room, for one night, without breakfast

PRICE CATEGORIES RESTAURANTS

Expensive   over 40 pounds

Moderate   17–40 pounds

Budget   under 17 pounds

The prices are for a three-course meal without drinks

On the cover: Showcasing elegant Georgian architecture p. 63 | The city at Festival time p. 91

CONTENTS

Shopping → p. 58

Entertainment → p. 66

Where to stay → p. 74

Street atlas → p. 102

DID YOU KNOW?
Heart of Midlothian → p. 33
Keep fit! → p. 42
Relax & enjoy → p. 45
Books & films → p. 48
Gourmet restaurants → p. 54
Local specialities p. 56
Luxury hotels → p. 79
Budgeting → p. 95
Currency converter → p. 96
The rules of the game → p. 97
Weather in Edinburgh → p. 98

MAPS IN THE GUIDEBOOK
(104 A1) Page numbers
and coordinates refer to the
street atlas
(0) Site/address located off
the map
Coordinates are also given for
places that are not marked on
the street atlas
A public transportation route
map can be found inside the
back cover

INSIDE BACK COVER:
PULL-OUT MAP →

PULL-OUT MAP 📖
(📖 A–B 2–3) Refers to the
removable pull-out map

RVC
LEARNING
CENTRE

2 | 3

The best MARCO POLO Insider Tips

Our top 15 Insider Tips

INSIDER TIP **Let your Celtic hair down**

At the Beltane Fire Festival held on the last day of April, more than 12,000 go on a pagan, Celtic spree that doesn't end until May. A really spectacular event on Calton Hill → p. 90

INSIDER TIP **Knights of the Thistle**

The Chapel of the Scottish Order of the Thistle in St Giles Cathedral is decorated with oak stalls for 16 knights and three members of the royal family, unusual coats-of-arms and angels playing bagpipes → p. 38

INSIDER TIP **William Turner likes it gloomy**

The National Gallery only exhibits some of the artist's watercolours in the weak January light to prevent them from fading even more → p. 43

INSIDER TIP **Parade in tails**

Your children will love Edinburgh Zoo; especially if they don't miss the daily penguin parade (photo right) → p. 88

INSIDER TIP **Roasting Scots**

It's no secret with the locals, but most visitors don't know about it: Edinburgh has its very own sandy beach → p. 47

INSIDER TIP **Cryptic crypt**

Non-stop horror films, pole dancing, cosy corners and 'candlelight burgers' in the gloomy Banshee Labyrinth under a bridge in the Old Town → p. 68

INSIDER TIP **Breathtaking panorama**

You will get the best photo of the castle from St Cuthbert's Cemetery at the foot of the hill. It is particularly beautiful in winter when leaves do not block your view → p. 45

INSIDER TIP **Dessert with a steely soft drink**

Irn-Bru, the orange-coloured Scottish pick-me-up and national soft drink is the basis of one of the desserts served in the Hotel du Vin Bistro → p. 54

INSIDER TIP **A hat to suit every head**

For men, it could be Sherlock Holmes' deerstalker cap; for ladies, definitely the mere wisp of a fascinator to decorate their hair – a milliner rules over her realm in the Fabhatrix in the heart of the Old Town → p. 62

INSIDER TIP **The local bus to the Da Vinci Code**

Bus lines 15 and 62 will take you in comfort, in half an hour, to the legendary, exquisite Rosslyn Chapel to the south of the city centre. Do you think you will be able to find the Holy Grail that some people think is hidden inside its walls? You can buy expert literature at the Chapel that will do away with many of the myths (photo left) → p. 80

INSIDER TIP **Ceilidh means party**

The people of Edinburgh have storytelling and music-making in their blood. They celebrate Gaelic culture at the Ceilidh Culture Festival at Easter – all washed down with plenty of drink, of course! → p. 90

INSIDER TIP **Checked nylons**

They really exist: tights with tartan patterns – on the Royal Mile. The square check powder pink model is even quite sexy → p. 63

INSIDER TIP **Feel at home**

You can rent a holiday flat behind the thick walls on Candlemaker Row – in the midst of the hustle and bustle of the Old Town near Greyfriars' Cemetery with its tales of vanishing corpses → p. 78

INSIDER TIP **Forward looking**

The large clock on the tower next to Waverly Station is two minutes fast so that passengers won't miss their train – the only exception is on New Year's Eve → p. 44

INSIDER TIP **Seaweed brew**

You will be able to try a drink you have definitely never had before at the David Bann vegetarian restaurant: beer made of seaweed → p. 55

BEST OF ...

GREAT PLACES FOR FREE
Discover new places and save money

● *Three-hour declaration of love to the city*
You will have certainly fallen in love with Edinburgh after this free tour of the metropolis. The enthusiastic guides are devoted to their city and know absolutely everything about haunted houses and spitting, inventions and striving for independence, about music making, etc, etc, etc. ... → p. 36

● *Secret Festival favourite*
Originally, the *Festival Fringe* was just an offshoot of the Edinburgh International Festival. But, for some years now, visitors have not only been attracted to the many comedy and theatre performances just because they're free (photo) → p. 91

● *First the sheep and then the kilt*
Do you want to find out how a kilt is made? The *Tartan Weaving Mill & Exhibition* will provide you with all the answers → p. 37

● *Scotland in session*
The Parliament Building looks like an upturned ship but this visionary construction fits perfectly into the tightly-knit Old Town. You can satisfy your curiosity about the cryptic architecture on a free tour → p. 37

● *Edinburgh's famous writers*
Burns, Scott and Stevenson are shining stars in the Scottish literature firmament. The memorabilia in the small *Writers' Museum* will give you an idea of the time they spent in Edinburgh → p. 39

● *Modern art from Scotland's capital*
Dean Gallery pays homage to Edinburgh's greatest artist – Eduardo Paolozzi: sculptor, Surrealist, Pop-Artist. The fascinating, modern artistic environment is continued into the café area, too → p. 47

● *Jazz for free*
The *Jazz Bar* swings more than any other club in town. From Tuesday to Saturday evening, free, un-plugged sessions go along with the first beer of the day at the bar's 'Teatime Acoustics' events → p. 72

◯◯◯◯● Dots in guidebook refer to 'Best of ...' tips

● *The castle on the volcano*

The most impressive aspect of *Edinburgh Castle* and the volcanic rock it is built on, is the silhouette the two merge to form. Things are more intimate inside the castle: crown jewels, the Stone of Destiny and a simple chapel are true gems. The views are breathtaking! → p. 30

● *Memento mori*

The gloomy *Greyfriars' Cemetery* in the heart of the Old Town is like a history book of the city carved in stone. A lot of people come here because they believe the place is haunted. The corpse thieves Burke and Hare dug up bodies buried here for an anatomy professor → p. 32

● *Fiddles in the bar*

Sandy Bell's is a pub with a resounding reputation. There is nothing more typically Scottish than listening to folk musicians at a jam session with a glass of beer in your hand → p. 72

● *Eating in the heart of the city*

You will feel like you are in a catacomb in the vaults of the *The Grain Store* restaurant. Tuck into the unpretentious food served by candlelight in what was once a warehouse → p. 56

● *Just a department store?*

Jenners, from 1838, does not try to be modern. Here a small escalator, there a narrow, winding staircase. You can never be quite sure which of the 100 departments on the six floors you will find yourself in – but Jenners sells absolutely everything (photo) → p. 61

● *Farmer's market with a view of the castle*

The best market in the country is quite simply named *Farmer's Market*. Sixty farmers and producers offer their exquisite, out of the ordinary, produce for sale on Saturday: wild boar, organic beer, ostrich and water-buffalo meat, lobster, honey, chutneys ... → p. 62

● *Bar on the bridge*

North Bridge has established itself in the foyer of the Scotsman newspaper. Where drinking used to inspire writers, the lovely bar now whets one's appetite for Edinburgh: pure *grandezza* → p. 79

ONLY IN

BEST OF ...

AND IF IT RAINS?
Activities to brighten your day

● *Play of light in the Cathedral*
The play of light created by the glass windows and modern glass curtain behind the entrance to *St Giles Cathedral* will even fascinate you if the weather is typically Scottish. Tours provided as well as organ music → p. 38

● *The haunted lane underneath the pavement*
Real Mary King's Close is the lane to end all lanes. This piece of the city's history is underground today and gives an authentic and gruesome impression of how life was in the Middle Ages → p. 86

● *Classicist temple of the arts*
The Classicist *National Gallery of Scotland* shows world-famous works alongside Scottish highlights. It is worth visiting the Gallery just to see Henry Raeburn's fabulous painting 'The Skating Minister' → p. 43

● *What a ship!*
Rule Britannia, Britannia rule the waves – the royal yacht, with its Art Deco interior, is no longer in service and is now anchored at Leith. A sensual feast for the eyes with the flair of the seas (photo) → p. 48

● *At the preacher's house*
John Knox was the rhetorical spearhead of the Scottish Reformation and Mary Stuart's opponent. His house is the most splendid on the Royal Mile and you can listen to the disputes between the preacher and Catholic queen while you visit it → p. 33

● *Take the train to the Aquarium*
Not only children will love the *Deep Sea World* underwater zoo – especially if you travel there by train from Waverly Station across the famous Firth of Forth Bridge → p. 88

RAIN

RELAX AND CHILL OUT
Take it easy and spoil yourself

● *Seduced by a chocolate Buddha*
Sumptuous, sinful, seductive – you should take some time out at *The Chocolate Tree* boutique to try the ginger Buddhas coated in cocoa or Venetian masks that melt in your mouth → **p. 51**

● *An evening view from the volcano*
You will have the most beautiful view if you look down on the city from the Greek columns on *Calton Hill* at twilight. Don't forget the sundowner → **p. 41**

● *Classical music in the church*
The *Greyfriars Kirk* has been through a lot; it was even a gunpowder warehouse in the 18th century and immediately blew up! It is now considerably more peaceful in the beautifully restored interior. The regular concerts of classical music are particularly atmospheric → **p. 33**

● *Just like home*
The living-room lounge *Underdogs* is a bit like a party cellar with sofas scattered around and dim lighting. Ideal for a drink before or after dinner → **p. 70**

● *Elegant living*
You will really be able to relax in one of the spacious flats behind the historical façade of the *Chester Residence*. There is round-the-clock service to take care of your every wish → **p. 76**

● *The pool above town*
Go up to the roof of the *Sheraton Grand*. Here you will be able to unwind in a spa with a panoramic view of the city → **p. 45**

● *Oasis of green in the city*
The *Princes Street Gardens* on the south side of the Old Town are Edinburgh's solarium. The former waste-water lake twinkles like a turquoise-coloured gem under the bold skyline of the Old Town – *dolce far niente*! (photo) → **p. 44**

INTRODUCTION

DISCOVER EDINBURGH!

As a small capital city on the edge of Europe, Edinburgh cannot play first fiddle in the global city orchestra – at the most, it could play first bagpipe. Many visitors often consider the city as the gateway to the Highlands. But, with its reputation as a capital city fully restored following the partial autonomy of Scotland in 1999 and the establishment of a regional parliament, this sleeping beauty started to awaken from its years of slumber. Its cultural festivals have now been joined by new restaurants with Michelin stars, fashion houses and boutiques, the revamping of the port and one of the most sensational parliament buildings in Europe. Direct flights from many European airports have made Edinburgh a perfect destination for an urban holiday.

This city is a real natural talent. Volcanism and the Ice Age left a dramatic hilly landscape behind them in this inlet on the Firth of Forth; but that would not really have such an effect without the city in the middle of it. A royal castle from the 7th century, perched like an eyrie on a hill, marked its beginnings, and the city started to develop around Edinburgh Castle – which rises high into the sky above the city. Seen from

Photo: The New Town with Princes Street Gardens

one of the three hills in the city, the dramatic skyline of the Old Town at sunset, or looming up out of the fog, creates one of the most atmospheric portraits of any European metropolis.

Bloody battles, wild legends and the cult of the kilt

Edinburgh – and Scotland – have one man in particular to thank that this remote beauty on the edge of the Highlands did not remain a place known only to insiders over the past 200 years. In the 19th century, the author Walter Scott took a story of a not terribly imposing man-at-arms and wove legends, bloody battles between the English and the Scots, and tragic love stories from the Highlands into a web of historical novels. The prose that flowed from Scott's pen is possibly not the most refined, but readers throughout Europe couldn't get enough of it. And, they started travelling to Scotland. Writers from the Continent felt that Edinburgh's Neoclassicist architecture invested it with the aura of an 'Athens of the North'. Scottish tourism and Hollywood's *Highlander* films would be inconceivable without Scott. The same applies to the cult of the kilt. Scott turned the skirt-like piece of clothing worn by the Highlanders – that had become scorned after an inglorious defeat by the English – into a fashionable garment when he invited King George IV to Edinburgh in 1822 and put him in a kilt, too.

Edinburgh's plus points are not limited to its magnificent location, historical novels and tartans. The authoritarian church reformer John 'Killjoy' Knox brought Calvinism to Catholic-oriented Edinburgh in 1560 and subjected the nation to his 'Book of Discipline'. Edinburgh became the epicentre of a Scottish moral earthquake that made the church more independent from the Crown – in contrast to England where the Reformation was more of a grass-roots affair. Edinburgh's Protestantism created institutions such as autonomous churches, law courts and schools.

Of course, the city, with around 50,000 inhabitants living in cramped conditions in ten-to-twelve storey buildings in the 17th century, stank to high heaven. If you threw your tankard at the wall of a pub, or so it is said, it would stick to the filth on it. In spite of this, an increasing number of poets and philosophers met in such pubs for a heated exchanges of ideas. The new Protestant philosophy created a resident of Edinburgh who, as a hot-headed Highlander, could never resist joining in a bar room brawl but still racked his brains over God and the world around him. The Scottish Age of Enlightenment resulted in the first faculty of medicine in Great Britain being established in Edinburgh in 1726, followed by a philosophical society in 1739. In Voltaire's opinion, the city was one of Europe's main intellectual centres for a time. Edinburgh was the home of many great intellectuals including Adam Smith, the father of economic theory – even though bankrupt Scotland had become almost powerless and the kingdom united with England in 1707.

If you plan a romantic evening picnic on Calton Hill, you will have Edinburgh and its (hi)story spread out to your left. In the background, the old castle with the densely populated medieval Old Town sweeping down from the hill top to the Palace of Holyroodhouse. On the right, a 'new', completely different and surprisingly well-ordered city comes into view – even though it is also a good 200 years old now. The Georgian New Town represents the *non plus ultra* of city planning of the period: uniform, precise, spacious and

> ## The city with two faces – Dr. Jekyll and Mr Hyde

fashionable – a wonderful place for a stroll and to see what is going on. Enormous windows and high rooms. Terrace houses and palatial façades. When Walter Scott invited the English king, George IV, to Edinburgh, he came into the New Town. This is where the better-off citizens had settled to get away from the overcrowding in the narrow streets and houses on the other side of town that had been there for centuries.

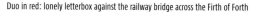

Duo in red: lonely letterbox against the railway bridge across the Firth of Forth

POST

3.45pm

However, there has been little architectural development of note in Edinburgh since the construction of the New Town around 1800 and the draining of the sewage-filled lake where Princes Street Gardens are today. A triumph like that was good enough for centuries.

With a population of approximately 450,000, Edinburgh is Scotland's second-largest city today. While the largest, Glasgow – only an hour away by train – appears post-industrial and shirt-sleeved, the bankers and civil servants in the capital seem to prefer suits and ties. The millennium politics of the London Scot Tony Blair made it possible for Scotland to break away from its political union with England. The Catalan architect Enric Miralles, now deceased, was allowed to build a fascinating parliament building in the Old Town; this created an eastern boundary to the already-existing row of houses when it was completed in 2004. Many of the people of Edinburgh complained that the building was too expensive but the architectural world was enthralled.

The Scottish Parliament is located near the Baroque Palace of Holyroodhouse, the Queen's residence when in the Scottish capital. The contrast between the two buildings makes one aware of the difficulties involved integrating contemporary design in a homogeneous environment. The building, in which the Scottish National Party (SNP) – with their sights firmly set on Scottish independence – still only swings the sceptre of partial autonomy, is not intended as a house for Scotland as a new state. At the moment, it seems that it has also provided the incentive for the extensive re-development of the area between the Royal Mile and Calton Hill.

Glasgow has already fought its way out if its industrial decline but Edinburgh still appears to be carefully working on plans to develop a more contemporary profile in the coming years. City planners have to steer a course between demolition and the demands of a World Heritage Site seeing that both the New and Old Town bear this coveted Unesco title. It come as no surprise that the Scottish capital with its two hearts is always on the brink of a cardiac arrest during the cultural festival month of August when more than 2 million visitors make the city burst at the seams. The creative urge to foster the human spirit which has not let the people of Edinburgh come to rest since the Enlightenment, erupts with full force in the Edinburgh International Festival, the Fringe Festival and the Military Tattoo. The International Festival has been the highlight of the summer in Edinburgh since 1947 and has been imitated by many other cities around the world.

It is fairly easy to explore the Scottish capital on foot – if you don't get lost. You will find yourself continuously going up and down hills and steps, and over rough cobblestones. Take sturdy shoes with you. Strolling around the carefully laid-out streets in the New Town is an easy affair but the Old Town is almost reminiscent of one of the impossible staircase constructions in drawings by the Dutch artist Maurits Cornelis

Climb up or take a break? Summer-time questions at the Scott Monument

Escher. Don't hesitate to ask locals the way – this could lead to a shortcut through a romantic cemetery. In conversation with the residents of Edinburgh, you will be able to listen to the delights of the Scottish accent with its almost uncontrollable rolled vowels – an accent that has stumped many a foreigner. It has a lovely ring to it and is nowhere nearly as difficult as Glaswegian. However, if you arrive in a pub while there is a music session in full swing, it might be that you will not understand anything at all. In that case, you will have hit on Gaelic singing. And what a stroke of luck. You will have come across the true Scottish soul of Edinburgh somewhere in the catacombs of the capital.

> **The magic of Edinburgh never fades**

This metropolis, which is both grotesquely Gothic and classically hip, has an enchanting air about it unlike virtually any other. And just when you start thinking about leaving this magic behind you, you will hear the sound of bagpipes echoing down the streets. So don't even try to entertain such thoughts: you can pack your bags whenever you want, check out of your hotel and set off for home – but Edinburgh will never really let you out of its spell!

WHAT'S HOT

1 A feast for the eyes

DRILL HALL

Drink in the atmosphere at Edinburgh's new arts café in The Out of the Blue Drill Hall. Relax with a fair trade ?s of wine or cup of coffee ? taking in an exhibition ?rmance. Enjoy freshly local produce unde? ?stic sweep of t? ?t with over ?at this ? ?nve? ?tre

Café and art Gastronomy and arts form a perfect symbiosis in *The Art Centre Café*. Everything is first rate and will make you want more *(1–3 Market Street)*. Not only artists who have their studios there get together in the *Drill Hall Arts Café*. You can really feel the creativity in the air *(36 Dalmeny Street)*. And, not only the kitchen is creative at *Henderson's*; the vegetarian restaurant also has its own gallery *(4 Thistle Street NW Lane)*.

Adventurous

2

Sport with an adrenalin boost See a landmark from a different perspective and go abseiling on the *Forth Rail Bridge (www.ultimateabseil.com, photo)*. The summer Rat Race – Urban Adventure Run has kayaking and climbing on the agenda alongside abseiling *(www.ratraceadventure.com)*. Orientation skills are demanded in *Braidburn Valley Park*. In orienteering, a course with 21 control points has to be passed – in the fastest time possible. The start is at the main entrance to the park on Greenbank Crescent *(www.braidburnvalley park.or.uk/orineteering)*.

On the pitch

3

3D football The Scots are not as wild about football as their neighbours to the south but are still interested in it. If you can't go to a match yourself, you can now watch it in 3D. The *Sportster's Bar* was a pioneer in this field and now boasts 30 screens *(1A Market Street, photo)*. The *Aspen Bar* also shows major sporting events in 3D *(66 South Bridge, www.baraspen.co. uk)*. You will almost feel like you are in the midst of the action in the *Volunteer Arms (180 Leith Walk)*. Other 3D sports bars under: *www.3dtvpubfinder.com*

Green sports

A workout for do-gooders Weeding, sowing, raking – they all require perseverance. And that is what the *Wester Hailes Health Agency* recognised. Every Tuesday, it organises a get-together to work in the garden and toughen up participants' muscles *(40 Drumbryden Drive, www.whhealth agency.org.uk)*. Is cycling a green sport? Of course; but the *Pedals* bike shop makes it even more environmentally friendly. The shop, which is furnished with recycled furniture, repairs bikes rather than disposing of them and ☺ uses biodegradable lubricants and as many used spare parts as possible to achieve this *(39 Barclay Place, www-pedals-edinburgh.com)*. Can you imagine a fitness studio being awarded a prize for animal protection? This happened to the *600 Plus Gym Spa* that provides a natural habit for numerous animals on its property *(2202 Cornerstone Boulevard, 600plusgymspa)*.

Tried and true

Vintage fashion They are more than just a passing fad: the small, exquisite shops in the city centre are a way of life. Not only do clients rediscover trends that have survived the passing of time they also invest in a good cause when they shop at *Bernardo's Vintage*, which used to be known as the Salvation Army *(116 West Bow, www. bernardos.org)*. *Godiva* not only has cool second-hand things to wear but also clothing from the *Edinburgh College of Art* – in this way, you can support up-an-coming designers *(9 West Port, www.godivaboutique.co.uk, photo)*. You will find unconventional clothing at *Herman Brown* that specialises in fashion from the 1970s and 1980s *(51 West Port, www.hermanbrown.co.uk)*.

IN A NUTSHELL

BAGPIPES

There are strong differences of opinion about the sounds that come out of these squawking, bellicose bags that are still played in many armies. Here, fact and myth clash – something typically Scottish. After the final battle for Scotland in Culloden in 1745, pipers were sentenced to death because the court martial classified bagpipes as weapons. This led to the rumour that the English would impose the death penalty on anybody playing the pipes.

That there were not enough pupils at piping schools had more to do with the fact that the clan chieftains had become too impoverished to pay for lessons. And that, even in modern day Edinburgh, cases actually come to court of people accused of disturbing the peace, is also true. In a bizarre case, a piper in London had to pay a fine for noisemaking. The court refused to accept that the death penalty, imposed on a piper in 1745, could be taken as a precedent and ruled that the bagpipe was indeed a musical instrument. The plaintiff, who saw his bagpipes more as a weapon, decided not appeal when the judge informed him that the alternative would be to be charged with the illegal possession of arms! The traditional Highland bagpipes are played using a

Where top spies deliver milk, men wear skirts and queens end up in prison – Edinburgh is all that and much more

nine-note scale. The bag is made of leather or occasionally Gore-Tex. They were already used by the Romans and today there are still dozens of different varieties of these shepherds' pipes around the world. This powerful noise-maker (130 decibels!) has many differ-ent names – some, such as the Finnish *säkkipilli*, are just as weird as the sound the instrument produces.

SEAN CONNERY

James Bond was born in Edinburgh in 1930. As a lad, Sean Connery delivered milk in the district around the famous Fettes College, which can boast having Tony Blair as one of its graduates and where the novelist Ian Fleming had his top spy educated. Connery became a bodybuilder, nude model at the Edinburgh Art College, and came in third at the 1950 Mister

Tartan kilts in step at the famous Military Tattoo

Universe Competition. He made his first film in 1956 and his most recent (as a virtual figure and voice in the animated film 'Sir Billi the Vet') in 2006. The first Bond actor never gave up his Scottish accent in his films. He was knighted by the Queen and, at the age of 69, the Century magazine elected him the *Sexiest Man of the Century*. He is a staunch supporter of the Scottish National Party (SNP).

CURRENCY

Strictly speaking, Scottish pound notes are not legal tender. In spite of this, the Scottish version of the British pound accounts for around 95 percent of payments. In contrast to the way things are done south of the border, the three largest Scottish banks distribute the banknotes. The three sets have different designs showing bridges, castles and famous Scots. The most-printed portrait is that of Sir Walter Scott. It is often difficult to pay with these notes – in denominations between 5 and 100 pounds – outside Scotland. Scotland does not mint its own coins. With a bit of luck, you might get hold of one of the Scottish one-pound notes that have now become rare – so keep it as a souvenir!

GREEN AGE

If the country's political intentions come true, Scotland's resurrection could be seen as the dawn of a new era of ecological awareness. Particularly because almost euphoric emphasis is being placed on the expansion of renewable energy resources. As a tourist, you will hardly notice this green wave. Many hotels and guesthouse do not have double glazing and still stick to their old sash windows. The Scottish breakfast is full of fat and far from being considered a healthy way to start the day. However, the green oval sign of the Green Tourism Business Scheme is becoming increasingly common at the entrance to places to stay, sights, restaurants and public buildings. 'VisitScotland' introduced the green label in 1997 and it has now been expanded to include the rest of Great

Britain. With more than 700 members and candidates, over half of those with the certificate are located in Scotland. They have to pass a 150-point environmental check every two years. Those who are successful are given a gold, silver or bronze sign. Tourists can look for this kind of accommodation in Scotland on the Internet site: *guide.visitscotland.com*. The chefs in better restaurants use local products as much as possible and some menus in Edinburgh indicate the origin of the beef and seafood they serve. However, low-energy hotels and slow food are still a long way off.

INVENTORS

Following Scotland's union with England in 1707 and the increase in the country's prosperity, its inventive potential came to the fore. Just some examples: James Watt improved the first steam engines and became the motor of industrialisation. Tarring streets can be traced back to John McAdam, the teacher of the hard of hearing Alexander Graham Bell was the father of the telephone. Kirkpatrick Macmillan built the first bicycle, Joseph Lister pioneered disinfecting surgical instruments, Bowman Lindsay worked on the first light bulb. Charles Mackintosh developed waterproof clothing, John Boyd Dunlop invented air-filled tyres. Linoleum was the brainchild of Frederick Walton. And Alexander Fleming was awarded the Noble Prize for the discovery of penicillin.

There are reasons why such a small country was blessed with so many men of genius. As early as in 1546, the church reformer John Knox, who preached in St Giles Cathedral on the Royal Mile, propagated compulsory education for all. The high academic standards and inventiveness have survived to this day – in the development of microelectronics, energy production from wave power (Stephen Salter) and in scientific attempts at genetic manipulation – remember Dolly the cloned sheep from Roslin near Edinburgh?

All of this inventiveness will be brought back to you over a beer in the delightful *Café Royal Circle Bar (p. 68)* with its tiled painting from 1886 showing great minds – including James Watt, Benjamin Franklin and Michael Faraday – at the moment of inspiration.

MARY QUEEN OF SCOTS

Edinburgh's most famous VIP has been dead for more than 420 years. The beautiful Mary Stewart – born in Linlithgow Castle west of Edinburgh in 1542 – was named Queen of Scotland in the same year. At the age of six, she was banished to the French court to be married and receive her education. When she was nineteen, she returned home as a Stuart and, for the next six years, led a scandalous life in Edinburgh with several marriages, rapes and murder in her court. But the real scandal was her Catholicism coupled with her zest for life in the age of the Reformation. Her exile in England – after she had driven all the Protestant nobility out of their offices and the country – ended in the dungeons of her royal cousin Elizabeth I who had her beheaded after 19 years of political imprisonment.

SCOTLAND FOR THE SCOTS

Following the union with England in 1707, the Scots actually developed into more-or-less satisfied British citizens. More recently, several of the country's most successful politicians have held seats in the lower house in London; these included the two Labour prime ministers Tony Blair and Gordon Brown. However, various incidents led to the Scottish National party (SNP), founded in 1934, taking away votes from the established parties and affecting the

State-of-the-art architecture: the debating chamber in the Scottish Parliament

mood in the country. North Sea oil and Margaret Thatcher's conservative, polarising politics led to the, formerly not especially nationalistic, Scots thinking about a stronger form of autonomy, and in 1997 the majority voted in favour of an independent parliament. The Scotsman Blair made this possible – devolution was the key word – and the first session of the Scottish Parliament was held in Edinburgh in 1999. The Labour politician Donald Dewar was elected First Minister but died shortly afterwards and did not experience to opening of the fascinating new Parliament Building in Edinburgh in 2004. The public dispute over the high construction costs, and the modern architectural concept drawn up by the Catalan Enric Miralles, also reflected the unease many Scots felt about their newly-won autonomy, as well as the lack of a national identity after so many centuries. The SNP developed into the second-strongest Scottish party and, after 2007, the First Minister even came from its ranks, although Alex Salmond started governing with only 47 of a total of 129 seats. Politically, Edinburgh is a pro-European capital with liberal values. 😊 There is no questioning the orientation on wind energy and wave power: the SNP belongs to the Green faction in the EU Parliament. In May 2011, the SNP surprised everybody by gaining an absolute majority of 69 seats for the first time and Alex Salmond will remain the head of government in the Holyrood parliament until 2016.

SCOTTISH

Scottish English sounds like a dialect but, from a linguistic point of view, it is quite different: Scottish is precisely the English spoken throughout Scotland as the national language of education. *Scots*, on the other hand, is much more of a dialect and is spoken by around one third of the Scots – especially in the southern parts of the country. It is not a literary language as there are no rules for its spelling. Writers, such as the classic Robert Burns and the contemporary Irvine Welsh, write what is spoken as they hear it, phonetically. Scottish Gaelic – Celtic – is a completely different matter; it was brought to Scotland by Irish immigrants many centuries ago. No matter where you come from, you should not forget that Edinburgh is always pronounced with a Scottish rasp as 'Edinbarra'!

TARTAN & KILT

The Gaelic word *tartan* means a checked cloak made of woollen fabric, although some believe it has its origin in the French word *tertaine*, a type of cloth. Used as an adjective it can also allude to Scotland or the Scots as in the case of a *tartan tax*. The most famous piece of clothing that is made of it, has its roots in the old-Scandinavian word *kilt*. In the 17th century, the Scots discovered the checked tunic once worn by the Celts for themselves. Approximately 6 to 8 yards of single-width (26–30 inches), or 3 to 4 yards of double-width cloth (54–60 inches) are needed to make a modern kilt; the pattern is determined by the clan the wearer belongs to. The cool weather in Scotland makes wearing knee-high socks vital and a small knife, the Sgian Dubh, is traditionally tucked into the right one (or the left, if the wearer is left-handed). This was appropriate clothing for the poor inhabitants of the rough terrain of the Highlands that they were forced to give up after they lost the Battle of Culloden. But, from 1815, the kilt made a re-appearance and King George IV wore one when he visited Edinburgh in 1822. The patterns were registered and, since then, there has been no stopping the triumphant progress of the checked woollen fabric. Organisations such as Amnesty International, the Royal Family and even the Pope, who visited Edinburgh in 2010, have their own tartans. Men usually attend Scottish weddings in – sometimes borrowed – kilts. One question remains to be answered: what do they wear under the kilt? It can

happen that the questioner is embarrassed when the wearer does a cartwheel to cure his or her curiosity.

WHISKY

A document in the Edinburgh National Library proves it: in 1494, a certain John Cor ordered '8 bolls of malt to make aqua vitae'. The noble single malt – a whisky made at a single distillery from a mash that uses one particular grain – was introduced about 400 years later but disappeared from the market before showing up again around 1960 as a drink for connoisseurs. Single Malt Whisky now accounts for approximately ten percent of all Scotch sold. Edinburgh is the malt capital and one of the best places to hunt for your favourite drop is on the Royal Mile. By the way, the Scottish 'water of life' is called *uisge beatha* which was subsequently shortened to *whisky*. Whatever you do, do not confuse this with the Irish or American varieties of *whiskey* written with an 'e'.

WORLD HERITAGE SITE

The harmonious coexistence of two well-preserved, fundamental city-planning concepts led to Edinburgh being granted the status of a World Heritage Site in 1995. You will cover almost three miles if you want to walk along the entire borderline between the Old and New Towns. 75 percent of the buildings are protected monuments. Projects in the medieval old city, such as the construction of new hotels, led to concerns about the preservation of Edinburgh's unique skyline until Unesco's experts determined that the planned buildings would not endanger the city's status. Trams will once again run between Leith and the airport, as well as down Princes Street, in 2012. But, some residents of Edinburgh still feel that the overhead cables on Princes Street will spoil the view of the old city.

THE PERFECT DAY
Edinburgh in 24 hours

08:00am BREAKFAST IN THE NEW TOWN

Welcome to Edinburgh's two 'Old Towns' – a World Heritage Site. Start with breakfast in the exclusive New Town: in the fashionable Broughton district, you can either try a cooked Scottish breakfast at one of the window tables in the *Olive Branch* → p. 57 or eat continental style in the hip Italian café *Valvona & Crolla* → p. 52

09:00am MEET THE SCOTS

Fortified, set off through the New Town. Turn to the south with the volcanic *Calton Hill* → p. 41 on your left. You should definitely visit the *National Portrait Gallery* on Queens Street → p. 47 (photo left), which has been restored to its former glory following renovations completed in 2011. Behind the neo-Gothic façade you will see a 'who's who' of historical and contemporary Scottish VIPs captured in paintings, photographs and even videos.

10:00am UP-MARKET SHOPPING

St Andrew Square → p. 58 opens off a small side street on the other side of Queens Street. Since Edinburgh's political upgrading, this large square has developed into a real magnet for shoppers. The iconic *Harvey Nicols* department store → p. 60 opened its doors and top labels from around the world followed.

11:15am TAKE A STROLL

Window shopping! *George Street* → p. 63 offers a spectacular display of elegantly proportioned Georgian architectural gems, as well as a wonderful row of exclusive shops. The head of government and the Scottish *National Trust* for the protection of historical sites have their offices on *Charlotte Square* → p. 42 designed by Robert Adams in 1791. The Trust's café is a wonderful place to have a snack and you should also take time to look at the exhibition on life in the Georgian period. Follow two circular residential streets to the north until you reach the little *River Leith* → p. 82 (photo right). Stay on the left of the bank on this side and walk for around half an hour along the watercourse through the green 'canyon'. What a contrast when you climb up again to Queensferry Road and reach the West End a few minutes later with Edinburgh Castle on its steep rock towering up above.

Get to know the best of Edinburgh – right in the city centre, in a relaxed way and all in a single day

`00:15pm` UP TO THE CASTLE

A few yards along Princes Street, and then to the right to *St Cuthbert Cemetery* → p. 45; behind it, a steep path leads you through the western section of *Princes Street Gardens* → p. 44 to *Edinburgh Castle* → p. 30.

`01:00pm` MILESTONES

Many will perhaps want to give the castle a miss for the time being; the almost 1¼ mi long downhill *Royal Mile* → p. 35 is just too attractive. Is your stomach starting to rumble? *The Grain Store* → p. 56 is a superb choice for lunch. Then it's back to the Mile, an endless celebration of Scottish myths and tartan kitsch – but there are also many highlights you should have a look at: *St Giles Cathedral* → p. 38, the *John Knox House* → p. 33 and the new *Scottish Parliament* → p. 37 next to the *Palace of Holyroodhouse* → p. 35.

`04:30pm` INSIDER TIPS FOR THE LABYRINTH OF THE OLD TOWN

You cannot avoid going down tiny side lanes in Edinburgh. The detour via steep Victoria Street takes you up to *Grassmarket* → p. 58 where you will be able to buy second-hand clothes at *Armstrong's* → p. 62 (photo above), unique fashions at *Totty Rocks* → p. 64 and the Scottish 'water of life' in the *Whisky Shop* → p. 65.

`06:15pm` WHISKY, BEER AND WILD FOLK MUSIC

Sunset and the twilight hour beckons. Wander from the end of Princes Street over the grassy lava bumps up to East End. There are several monuments here including the columns of the unfinished *National Monument* → p. 42. You should enjoy the fabulous view of the skyline of the city and castle at sunset – and drink a toast of whisky from your hip flask while you do so. Take a taxi to *Sandy Bell's* pub → p. 72 or the *Royal Oak* → p. 72 for a beer and unplugged folk music. The nights there can be very long …

It is easy to explore Edinburgh's inner city areas on foot. With the *Edinburgh Pass*, you can use the bus network for up to three days which connects them with the suburbs.

SIGHTSEEING

CITY **WHERE TO START?**
It is easy to explore the Old and New Town on foot if you start at **Waverley Station (106 B6)** (*F4*). A flight of steps leads to the Royal Mile. The elegant shops on George Street and St Andrew Square in the New Town are also only a five-minute walk from Waverley. Underground car park at Waverley Station, New Street. From the airport: Airlink Bus 100 or – starting in 2012/13 – the tram to the airport from Waverley Station, Princes Street (30 min).

Edinburgh is like a stage set, not a modern metropolis. Climb up one of the three steep volcanic hills in the centre and you will see two completely different inner cities at your feet – from two periods – but hardly any modern architecture.

Seen from ☆ Edinburgh Castle, the urban drama that unfolds below could be a thriller in a romantic setting that has inspired writers in their creativity for centuries. Go down into the splendid theatre, make your entrance on stage, and become a performer and member of the audience at the same time.

Once you reach the bottom, everything is within easy walking distance – and there

Photo: View of the Old Town from the Scott Monument

Streets that breathe history in the Old Town – and urban elegance in the New Town: a contrasting picture of Edinburgh

is no need to rush. If you are in hurry, you will miss what is the most amazing aspect of the individual districts – their astonishing architectural homogeneity. Edinburgh has many intimate corners where you will quite tangibly feel what is lying beneath the surface of the city. So don't overlook any well-trodden stepped streets, don't miss a single cemetery, and grasp every opportunity to have a chat with the locals.

The urban compactness of the Old Town is only broken by the bridge that sweeps north to Edinburgh's main Waverly Station. The only breach in the phalanx of houses has been created by the Scottish Parliament Building – a modern, controversial architectural masterpiece – in the lower section of the Old Town.

However, Edinburgh can also appear quite arrogant at times; especially where

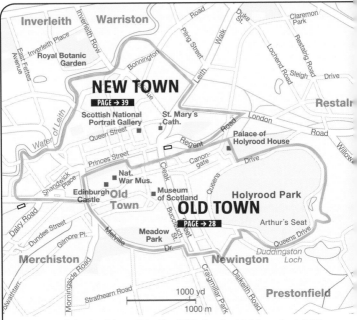

The map shows the location of the most interesting districts. There is a detailed map of each district on which each of the sights described is numbered.

the New Town seems to consciously show off its architectural uniqueness. You should walk through the gorgeous Princes Street Gardens on your way to the fascinating villa city from 1800. Robert Louis Stevenson grew up here in the Georgian New Town and he immortalised the hybrid nature of his hometown in his novel about the good-natured Dr. Jekyll who turned into Mr Hyde the murderer. In the end, you should leave the stage by the back door: to the west, you can then walk along the small river called the Water of Leith through a rustic idyll that runs down to the sea where the old port of Leith has now developed into a fashionable place to go out and have a good time, either during the day or in the evening.

OLD TOWN

The Royal Mile is where you will feel the real heartbeat and vivacity of Edinburgh all the way along its entire length of 5900 feet – the equivalent of an old Scottish mile.

Strolling up and down the Mile, a day will pass in no time; it slopes slightly to the east all the way from the castle to the Palace of Holyroodhouse. Between the two, shops in the medieval 'high-rises' do all they can to lure the crowds of tourists passing by with *kilts, tartans* and *whisky.* But, you will also discover small basement restaurants and cafés, churches, museums and lanes with steps that branch off the

Mile like ribs from the backbone. To the south, the streets appear more like canyons between the multi-storeyed listed buildings. Small, steep connecting lanes such as *Victoria Street*, *Candlemaker Row* and *King's Stables Road* lead like arteries into the lively, beating heart of the Old Town. There, any number of boutiques flourish between tap rooms, coffee-houses and restaurants. And a pulsating nightlife can be found in the medieval labyrinth of streets between *Grassmarket, Cowgate* and *Nicholson Street*.

■1 ARTHUR'S SEAT ☆
(111 F4) (*Ø J6*)

On a clear day, you can see more than 60 miles from the top of the most dramatic of the three volcanic hills in the city at a height of 823 ft. After around 320 ft, you will already have a fine view of the Parliament and, it is only from this perspective that you will be able to fully appreciate

how it was slotted into the old city. If you intend to make the five-mile hike of the heights, you should be sure to wear sturdy shoes and weatherproof clothing. You might be caught out by the quickly changing the weather and the rough terrain.

■2 CAMERA OBSCURA ☆
(109 F2) (*Ø E5*)

It fascinated Victorian tourists in 1850 and still attracts many visitors today. A kind of moveable pinhole camera with a focal length of 337.7 inches projects views of Edinburgh in the dark upper storey of a tower next to the castle. As if by magic, images of sections of the city with the gentle charm of old drawings appear before the visitors' eyes in the tower room. The exhibitions you see on the way upstairs, explain the context of the photographs. Modern telescopes have been set up on the roof of the Camera Obscura Tower to enable you to draw the New and Old

---

MARCO POLO HIGHLIGHTS

Towns up close. Interactive exhibitions in the magical tower explain visual phenomena such as holograms and plasma-energy. The Camera Obscura is more interesting when the weather is fine but the exhibitions are so absorbing that they will also help you forget a rainy day. *Daily April–Oct 9.30am–6pm, Nov–March 10am–5pm, July, Aug to 7.30pm | entrance fee £10.95 | Castle Hill | www.camera-obscura.co.uk*

3 EDINBURGH CASTLE ★ ● ☼
(109 E–F 2–3) *(ΩU D–E5)*

This castle is the highlight of any city tour and one you will really have to look up to; not because of its physical appearance but its exposed position on one of the three volcanic hills in the centre of the city. Castle Hill slopes steeply downwards on three sides but the Old Town finds its way

Heating like the knights of old in Edinburgh Castle

SIGHTSEEING IN OLD TOWN
1 Arthur's Seat
2 Camera Obscura
3 Edinburgh Castle
4 Greyfriars

gently into the valley on its eastern flank. It is difficult to imagine just how remote this castle must have looked when King Edwin of Northumbria in the north-east of England had this lonely fortress erected here; a fort on a hill – this is the Celtic translation of Edinburgh; but some argue that it could mean Edwin's fort. After this, kings were fathered and born here, prisoners locked in the dungeons and guests even assassinated.

The two freedom fighters William Wallace (1270–1305) and King Robert the Bruce (1274–1329) have taken up position at the

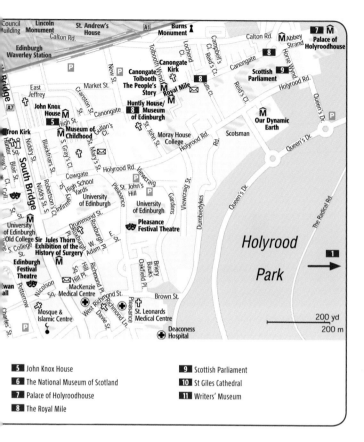

entrance, the *Gatehouse* built in 1887. In summer, you will hardly be able to get a good look at them; there will be so many other visitors behind you pushing to get in. Shortly after passing the bottleneck at the *Portcullis Gate*, you will find yourself standing in front of the two main attractions inside the castle: one of them is the enormous *Mons Meg Cannon* – probably produced in Mons in Belgium in 1457, it weighs 6 tons and could shoot stone cannonballs with a diameter of 20 inches weighing 150 kg. It was fired for the last time in 1681. Today, a modern 4.1 inch

weapon lets off a shot everyday – except Sunday – at 1pm, a lot of people working down below in the city call this the 'lunchtime bang'. Be sure to cover year ears if you are there when it goes off! In the 19th century, sailors in the port outside the city used to use this to adjust their chronometers.

The other highlight is *St Margaret's Chapel* from the 12th century. It was possibly built by King David I; Robert the Bruce laid his claim to the throne based on his descent from the former monarch. The elegant, unpretentious chapel with the slightly

There is no better site for a castle and none is more impressive: Edinburgh Castle

asymmetrical layout still has a touching effect on today's visitors, even though the interior has unfortunately been whitewashed.

The Scottish crown jewels from the early 16th century – the crown, created by James Mossmann *(see: John Knox House)*, the sceptre and sword – were simply stored in a chest in the castle after the realisation of the union with England in 1707 but are now once again on display in the Crown Hall under the title of the *Honours of Scotland*. In 1996, they were joined by an even older – and, for Scots, much more important – ancient artefact, the Stone of Scone. The early kings of the Scots and Picts were crowned on this stone until the English seized it in 1296 and placed under the English Coronation Chair. The British Prime Minister John Major returned it 700 years later shortly before Scotland voted in favour of autonomy.

The rest of the castle is made up of a few barracks buildings but the really impressive thing is the view over the city and surrounding countryside. *Daily April–Sept 9.30am–6pm, Oct–March 9.30am–5pm | entrance fee £15 | Castle Hill | www.edinburghcastle.gov.uk*

4 GREYFRIARS ● (110 A3) *(Ⓜ F6)*

This is not the neatest cemetery in town but definitely the one with the most unique atmosphere and the most interesting for fans of spine-chilling and historic graves. One of the most unusual attractions for tourists is the small monument to a Skye terrier which guarded his master's grave for 14 years after his burial in 1858 until he finally died himself. However, the cemetery has much more to offer than famous Greyfriars Bobby. The first church after the Reformation was built here in 1620 and radical Presbyterians, the so-called covenanters, signed the *National Covenant (www.covenanter.org)* at this historical site in 1638. The document was the Reformation's counter-concept for a radical, religious, socio-democratic response to the royal Episcopalian Church and was intended to establish the independence of the Presbyterian Church. If you look carefully among the sombre, monumental gravestones, you will come across a memorial stone to the covenanters who were persecuted and executed in the days of religious dispute. Today, there are no traces of the damage caused by fire and a devastating gunpowder explosion in the *Greyfriars Kirk* which is now also the venue for regular ● classical music concerts.

Greyfriars is also a permanent feature on many spine-tingling tours; the cemetery inspired the two Irishmen William Burke and William Hare to their career as cold-blooded body snatchers. In 1827, they started earning their money by digging up recently buried bodies and selling them to the then famous Anatomical Institute for 10 to 12 pounds for each intact corpse. However, most of the deliveries for use in Professor Knox's lectures came from at least 16 murders they had

committed. A crowd of 20,000 witnessed Burke's hanging at Lawnmarket in 1829; Hare testified as a state witness and avoided execution. *Corner Candlemaker Row and Chambers Street | www.greyfriarskirk. com*

⬛5 JOHN KNOX HOUSE ●
(110 B2) (*m̂ G5*)

This 500-year-old historic house is definitely the most visually attractive building on the Royal Mile. John Knox, the founder of Scottish Presbyterianism, may possibly have lived in the building and this saved it from being demolished in 1830. It is certain, however, that the rich goldsmith James Mossmann actually did live here and that he safeguarded his home by having an entrance on the first floor, stairs that are difficult to negotiate and false locks. His contemporary, Knox, was inspired by the religious reformer Johannes Calvin in Geneva and set out to reform Scotland's church.

You enter the rooms where the faded original ceiling paintings and some furniture from the Knox and Mossmann era give an authentic atmosphere, via a spiral staircase. While you look out of the window at what is happening on the Royal

HEART OF MIDLOTHIAN

A large mosaic heart in the tarmac near the west portal of St Giles Cathedral and not far from the former parliament – today, a law court – can easily go unnoticed. But every resident of Edinburgh knows it and some still spit on it as has been customary since the 15th century. This used to be the site of a prison and decapitated heads were displayed on spikes here. The locals used to protest by spitting in front of the prison gate. Walter Scott mentioned the gruesome prison in his novel *The Heart of Midlothian* (1818) and this is somewhat to blame for all the spitting! One of Edinburgh's football clubs is named after the novel's title and so fans of the local rival team, the Hibernians, also spit on the heart. *High Street, Royal Mile*

He wasn't as fragile in real life: a glass window with a picture of John Knox

Mile, you will suddenly hear debates Knox had with Mossmann and Mary Queen of Scots. The Catholic Queen of Scotland, who had been educated in France, and the strict, quarrelsome religious teacher often clashed with each other, particularly over her loose lifestyle. However, it should be mentioned that the democratic church reformer and father of several daughters was generally suspicious of woman as shown in his treatise 'The First Blast of the Trumpet against the Monstrous Regiment of Women'.

At the time, John Knox was considered a magically convincing speaker. The *Scottish Storytelling Centre* attached to John Knox House furthers rhetoric and the widespread Scottish pleasure at the art of telling tales. There is an interactive 'Scotland's Stories' exhibition in the cheerful rooms with the pleasant café – a real contrast to the labyrinthine part of Knox's house. There are INSIDER TIP storytelling events in the evening *(July, Aug Wed 7pm, monthly at other times | entrance fee £4)* where tales are read or made up going along. This is a good introduction to literary Edinburgh and Scotland. There are also city tours with storytelling guides *(from £6). Mon–Sat 10am–6pm, July, Aug also Sun noon–6pm | entrance fee £5; Scottish Storytelling Centre: free | 43 High Street, Royal Mile | www. scottishstorytellingcentre.co.uk*

6 THE NATIONAL MUSEUM OF SCOTLAND (110 A–B3) (*ꭐ F6*)

Two in one – the more than 120-year-old Victorian Royal Museum and the National Museum that opened around a decade ago have joined forces. The convex-shaped, dazzling sandstone façade of the new building opposite the mysterious, mossy Greyfriars Cemetery creates a fascinating visual contrast in the cityscape.

Inside, Scotland presents itself in all its facets: the blade from Edinburgh's guillotine, illuminating information on Dolly the genetically-manipulated sheep that was cloned just 6 miles away in Roslin, stuffed animals and skeletons, minimalist fashion creations designed by Jean Muir who died in 1995 – she had Scottish parents – and the supposed relics of St Columba, the Irish-Celtic monk who converted the Scottish Picts to Christianity in the 5th century, along with many objects from the world of technology. A hybrid museum that never ceases to amaze its visitors. After the visit, you can fortify yourself in the INSIDER TIP *Tower Restaurant in the new building (daily noon–11pm | tel. 01312 25 30 03 | www.towerrestaurant.com | Moderate)* – try the smoked-eel tempura – with a view of the city centre and the castle. *Daily 10am–5pm | Chambers Street/corner Candlemaker Row | www.nms.ac.uk*

7 PALACE OF HOLYROODHOUSE

(107 D–E 5–6) (H4)

The Royal Mile becomes really regal at the bottom. Seeing that there is (currently) no Scottish king, the English monarch has to come by once a year to air the palace. Without that, Holyroodhouse – which looks more like a stately home than a palace – would possibly once again fall into the poor state it was in when the young composer Felix Mendelssohn-Bartholdy saw it in 1829: dilapidated, without a roof, overgrown with ivy. The musician stated that this had inspired him to the somewhat lugubrious oboe melody at the beginning of his romantic 'Scottish Symphony'. It might be a good idea to listen to the work on your MP-3 player instead of the voice on the audio-guide when you make your way through the dozen or so rooms that can be visited. Some bedrooms and dining rooms are open to the public if the Queen is not in town. As with the castle, Holyroodhouse's history is what makes it really fascinating. When King David I was threatened with being horned by a stag while hunting, he had a vision of the Holy Cross between the animal's antlers and his tragic fate was warded off. After this, the King had the Augustine Order build a monastery to the Hoy Cross (Holy Rood); its ruins next to the palace invite visitors to take a stroll.

A visit to the palace is an absolute must for fans of historical conspiracy theories – this is where Mary Stewart's highly-educated Italian secretary David Rizzio was murdered in front of the pregnant Queen. The Catholic Mary Stewart, who had spent her youth in France and gallicised the name into Stuart, returned to an austere, Calvinist Edinburgh where she married her cousin Lord Darnley. He – as well as the Presbyterian clique of the nobility – found his wife's predilection for literature and singing not particularly Scottish. Rizzio the aesthete had to be done away with. Darnley himself was assassinated a little later; but, that is not part of the palace's history.

The fascinating mixture of the Scottish baronial style and elements of a French château develops a INSIDER TIP special charm in the evening when the setting sun lights up the palace's main façade. The rooms in the adjacent *Queen's Gallery* show changing exhibitions from the Royal Collection in Windsor Castle. *April–Oct daily 9.30am–6pm, Nov–March 9.30am–4.30pm | entrance fee £11; £16 with Queen's Gallery | Canongate, Royal Mile | www.royalcollection.org.uk*

8 THE ROYAL MILE ★

(110–111 A–D 2–1) (E–H 4–5)

It is said that around 60,000 people lived on the Royal Mile and the streets branching off of it – the so-called *closes* and *wynds* – in the 18th century; the highest population density in Europe at the time. The residential buildings, the *lands*, had as many as 15 storeys; the simple folk lived at the bottom and top while the better-off merchants and craftsman had their flats in between. The well-trodden steps on the left and right of the Mile can lead to picturesque courtyards – it is worth following them from time to time. Or you might unexpectedly topple over the threshold of a hidden pub and soon

famous Edinburgh philosopher and econ-omist David Hume (1711–76), a friend of the economics theoretician Adam Smith from the same town, seated in a classical pose. ● *Free tours* through the city start at 11am, 1pm and 3pm from *Tron Kirk* in the High Street *(www.getyourguide.com).* For many years, Canongate lay outside the

Blue skies over the Royal Mile – regal weather for pavement cafés

get into a chat with the locals at the bar over a lukewarm glass of top-fermented *ale*. But keep an eye open for guided ghost and street-ballad tours. Thank goodness, the ultimate horror has been done away with: today, nobody has to take cover when the bell of St Giles chimes 10 o'clock – fol-lowed by the warning cry of *'gardy luh'* (from the French 'gardez l'eau' – watch out, water!) – when the contents of all the chamber pots were emptied into the streets.
The Royal Mile is divided into three sections: *Lawnmarket, High Street* and *Canongate.* Lawnmarket boasts a monument to the

city boundary separated by the *Flodden Wall*; you can still see traces of this in the tarmac on the street between Greyfriars and the National Museum *(corner of Chambers Street/Forrest Road).* There is a statue of the talented poet Robert Fergusson who died at the age of 24 in 1754 in front of the small *Canongate Kirk* in the Canongate section (the Queen and other members of the Royal Family often attend services here when they are at the palace). When the life-sized statue of the vigorously striding poet was unveiled in front of thousands of spectators not far away from the parliament, an actor dressed up as Robert Burns leaped out of the crowd and declaimed some of Fergusson's verses.

You will also find traces of Fergusson in *Canongate Cemetery* where he is buried, as are Adam Smith and Mary Stuart's murdered secretary David Rizzio. Robert Burns, who was born 9 years after Fergusson, was greatly inspired by the young genius and donated his gravestone.

▣ SCOTTISH PARLIAMENT ★
(111 D1) (*ш H4–5*)

An exciting contrast in building styles awaits the visitor at the lower end of the Royal Mile. In Edinburgh, the Catalan architect Enric Miralles demonstrated how a modern building could find its place in the narrow sea of houses, many of which had been constructed centuries ago. Most people saw this as poetic architecture orientated on the geography of the Old Town and geology of Scotland while others complained that it was much too expensive. The international community acknowledges how utterly successful Miralles' building is. However, the architect died in 2000 at the young age of 45 before construction was completed in 2004 and could no longer explain one of the puzzling features of the Parliament; namely, the scale-like design of the rear windows.

There is a section where the astonishingly spacious building amalgamates with a house from 1685 *(Queensberry House)* making it possible for a ghost living there to participate in the meetings of parliament held from Tueday to Thuday. It is to be hoped that the political activities taking place within the building are just as transparent as the construction itself: the seating arrangement in the main debating chamber encourages dialogue in contrast to the confrontational layout in Westminster. It is possible to attend par-

liamentary meetings on Wednesdays and Thudays; free tickets for the Public Gallery can be ordered in advance by anyone interested and are much in demand *(tel. 0131 48 52 00 or 0800/0 92 71 00)*. There is also a very interesting ● **INSIDER TIP** one-hour tour on days when there are no meetings. If you don't want to take part in this, information is provided in an exhibition and you can go to the café. *April–Oct Mon, Fri 10am–6pm, Tue–Thu 10am–5pm, Sat, Sun 10am–4pm, Nov–March Fri–Mon 10am–4pm, Tue–Thu 9am–7pm | free admission | Canongate | www.scottish.parliament.uk*

LOW BUDGET

▶ There are coupons on the back of tickets of the city *Lothian Buses* that offer discounts for fast-food outlets and reduced admission to the Dungeons chamber of horrors.

▶ Admission to most of Edinburgh's museums is free! This also applies to the *Royal Botanic Garden* and the ● *Tartan Weaving Mill & Exhibition (daily 9.30am–5.30pm | 555 Castlehill, Royal Mile)* a *kilt* factory that shows all stages in the production of the multi-coloured cloth, from shearing the sheep to trying on the finished garment.

▶ There is no need to take a taxi back to your hotel after midnight – you can use one of the Night Buses. The ten lines are marked with an 'N' at most bus stops and some of them even travel as far as ten miles out of town *(night fare £3 | www.lothianbuses.com)*.

■10 ST GILES CATHEDRAL ●

(110 A2) (*M* F5)

St Giles does not seem very inviting at first glance. The compact building is almost overpowered by the phalanx of tall buildings from the late Middle Ages on the Royal Mile and you could possibly even walk past it if it was not for the charmingly playful pinnacles. And this, even though the High Kirk of St Giles is the Mother Church of Scottish Presbyterianism. It is actually not even a cathedral seeing that St Giles was only an Anglican Episcopal See for two short periods in the 17th century. The Church of Scotland has a democratic assembly of Presbyters instead of a strict hierarchy.

These are just a few aspects of the cathedral's very eventful history. Church services have been held here since 854 although the pillars around the altar from 1120 are now the oldest remainders of the building to have survived. The new building was erected in the Gothic style after its predecessor had been destroyed by the English. The severe Gothic dimensions must have pleased John Knox: it provided the perfect stage for the blazing sermons he delivered as pastor from 1560 to 1572. St Giles hardly came to rest later on either. Edinburgh's church history is characterised by countless intellectual conflicts on the true faith and appropriate building. The tour can be highly recommended.

The fascinating INSIDER TIP ▶ *Chapel of the Scottish Order of the Thistle*, built in 1911, is a real gem with its exquisite wood and stone carving. The national emblem of Scotland in the Order's name – the second highest British honour after the Order of

The first church service was held within the walls of St Giles Cathedral more than 1100 years ago

the Garter – is a clear indication as to why the majority of the 16 knights should be Scots. The Queen, as Sovereign, and the Duke of Edinburgh and the Princess Royal as additional knights and ladies, bring the number of members to 19. If necessary, the row of knights is made complete by royal appointment in November. Each knight has his own seat decorated with his coat of arms – commoners have to have one designed before they can be admitted to the Order – in the oak stalls. David Steel, the first president of the Scottish parliament, had a jaguar added to his metal shield; some people feel that he did this because he was so fond of the car with this name. King Olaf of Norway and the former Australian Prime Minister Robert Menzies were admitted to the order as extra members. The most peculiar decorations in the chapel are two angels playing bagpipes. *April–Sept daily 9am–7pm, Oct–March daily 9am–5pm | Lawnmarket, Royal Mile*

11 WRITERS' MUSEUM ●
(110 A2) (*ω E5*)

This building from 1622 is the only original house in the street leading off of the Lawnmarket section of the Royal Mile. Today, it is a museum commemorating the writer trio Burns, Scott and Stevenson. Early editions of their works are on display along with personal mementos including Burns' snuffbox. There is also a **INSIDER TIP** very cosy corner where you can settle down for a good read. Sometimes even modern authors are given exhibitions. *Mon–Sat 10am–5pm, in Aug also Sun noon–5pm | free admission | Lady Stair's Close Lawnmarket, Royal Mile*

NEW TOWN

The New Town could be described as Edinburgh's 'better half' where visitors no longer have to find their way through the narrow canyons of the Old Town with its pleasantly mysterious atmosphere, but can stroll at ease through a generous, bright rectangle of streets with uniform three-storey façades that was laid 200 years ago.

One regularly repeated architectural element is the semicircular fanlight over front doors. And rows of house façades and terraced town houses from the time when all of the kings were called George. Three long, main streets highlight the east-west axis. *George Street*, named after George III, dominates the scene from the ridge of a hill and seems to be the Georgian answer to the medieval Royal Mile. There are many top international – and especially London-based – fashion stores, café and nightclubs behind the large sash windows and in the basements. Shopping and window-shopping is a very relaxed affair here. It is interesting that INSIDER TIP Sunday is the most pleasant day to go for a stroll or shop anywhere in the New Town; this is when even Edinburgh's bankers and other workers unwind a bit and – well dressed, of course – go to cafés for a chat and to read their *Scotland on Sunday* newspaper.

A highlight of new elegance in an old town house can be seen the recently renovated *St Andrew Square* with every shopper's paradise, Harvey Nichols, at its east end. Further to the east, *St James Centre*, a shopping centre and office block built in the 1960s, shows what can happen when the good taste of the Georgian period of around 1800 is ignored. Plans

The life of Scotland's capital pulsates on Princes Street

SIGHTSEEING IN NEW TOWN

1 Calton Hill
2 Charlotte Square
3 Georgian House

are, however, afoot to give this a facelift one day. The heart of the New Town is bordered by *Princes Street* and *Queen Street* both sides of George Street. The two, somewhat narrower, Thistle and Rose Streets, named after the national flowers of Scotland and England, with their many inexpensive shops and pubs lie like mirror images between the three main streets. From the north-south axes that cross George Street at regular intervals, you look towards the Old Town on the one side, and the Firth of Forth inlet on the other. The New Town stretches northwards from Queen Street as far as *Fettes*

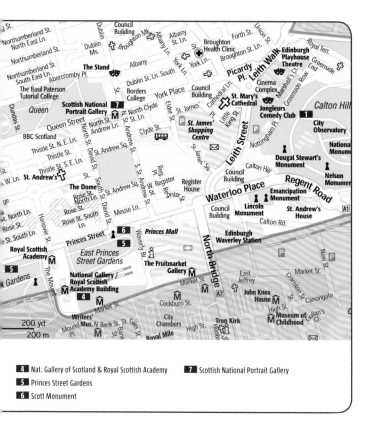

4 Nat. Gallery of Scotland & Royal Scottish Academy
5 Princes Street Gardens
6 Scott Monument

7 Scottish National Portrait Gallery

College, Edinburgh most famous independent school. The circular Georgian residential streets *Royal Circus, Moray Place* and *Ainslie Place* are three of the pearls in the crown of the New Town.

1 CALTON HILL ★ ● ☼
(106 C4–5) (*ⰙⰑ G3–4*)

Shortly before sunset, photographers haul their tripods up the hill, couples have cheese and wine – or even champagne – in their rucksacks. This is the **INSIDER TIP** best place in town to enjoy the twilight hour when the fading rays of the sun and the lights of the city merge with each

other. Balmoral Hotel and the castle are illuminated focal points; the traffic on Princes Street draws a line of light towards the west. The silhouette of the Old Town in front of Arthur's Seat dominates the view to the left and, to the right, the eye swings towards the port and Firth of Forth.

This is a view one cannot get enough of but it is also a strange kind of architectonic rendezvous. The area on the park-like hill is taken up by a disparate group of monuments that appear to have been placed here due to lack of space somewhere else. The twelve Doric columns designed by Edinburgh's Neoclassicist builder William

Henry Playfair were erected in 1822 as a *National Monument*. It was planned to be a bombastic war memorial but the necessary funding ran out; today this reminder of a Greek temple still touches the soul of any romantic person gazing up at it on the eastern horizon from Princes Street. Next to it, the 105 ft high tower of the ☀ *Nelson Monument* from the same period rises like an upright telescope *(April–Sept Mon 1–6pm, Tue–Sat 10am–6pm, Oct– March Mon–Sat 10am–3pm | entrance fee £4)*. 143 steps lead up to the most magnificent view of the city – a delight when there is not a strong wind. It is 4000 ft as the crow flies to the castle and that is exactly the length of the steel cable was that was stretched between the huge clock on the tower and the castle in 1861. It was intended to fire a cannon shot at exactly 1pm every day – as a signal for sailors in the port of Leith who could not see the clock tower when it was foggy. The monumental duo is complemented by Playfair's stocky *City Observatory*, as well as his small memorial temple – another Greek inspiration – for the Edinburgh moral philosopher Dugald Stewart (1753– 1828) and a monument to the local mathematician John Playfair (1748–1819). Further down the hill, you should take a stroll through the INSIDERTIP *Calton Cemetery* and past the terraces Playfair designed along the eastern slope of the hill. *www.cac.org.uk*

🔳 CHARLOTTE SQUARE ★
(109 D1–2) (*𝄞 D4–5*)

This spacious rectangle with its elegant façades at the west end of the New Town is the top address in Edinburgh – from a political point of view. The *Secretary of State for Scotland* resided in *house no. 6* until 1999. Today, it is the home of the head of the Scottish government – Alex Salmond, of the Scottish National Party, since 2007 – and brings a touch of London's 10 Downing Street to Edinburgh. As you walk past, you will get a feeling for the political and lobbying business in Edinburgh. However, the First Minister's home is no different from the other houses including the *Georgian House (no. 7)* that is now a museum.

In addition to the Georgian House, it is also possible to visit *house no. 28* on the other side of the square where the headquarters of the *National Trust for Scotland (NTS)* are located. Inside, tourists and the political and cultural elite rub shoulders in the busy café with its beautiful parquet floor. In summer, the elegant INSIDERTIP inner courtyard is a delightful place to have lunch. A visit to the exhibitions of Scottish paintings and furniture from the

KEEP FIT!

Just walking up and down the steps and steep streets of the Old Town should take care of average fitness requirements. The sloping profile of the city offers many interesting places for jogging: an early-morning run through the still deserted Princes Street Gardens below the castle is a wonderful experi- ence. In the New Town, the right bank of the River Leith offers a lovely run through the canyon and up steep streets to the centre. Even well-trained mountain runners will find what they are looking for here: the route from Holyroodhouse to Arthur's Street is very popular with the locals and also quite challenging.

18th and 19th centuries inherited by the NTS on the upper floor is well worthwhile. *No. 28* can be especially recommended to all those interested in the Georgian style and who find themselves standing in front of locked doors at the Georgian House in winter. *Gallery Mon–Fri 11am–3pm, shop, café-restaurant Mon–Sat 9.30am–5.30pm | 28 Charlotte Square | www.nts.org.uk*

Many famous people had Charlotte Square as their address; these include the inventor of the telephone Alexander Graham Bell, the founder of hospital hygiene Joseph Lister, as well as Field Marshal Douglas Haig, British Commander-in-Chief on the Western Front in World War I.

3 INSIDER TIP GEORGIAN HOUSE
(109 D1) (*ωι D4*)

This is the perfect place to find out about life in an upper-class Georgian home in Edinburgh. Form the outside, house no. 7 is a typical terrace house at the northern end of Charlotte Square with a (Neo) classicist, symmetrical façade in the style propagated by the architect Robert Adams. The uniformity of the layout continues on the inside where it also contrasts with the fascinating, cosy interior. Georgian taste could not tolerate any carpets on the floor in contrast to the later more pompous Victorian period. The kitchen and dining room are real eye-catchers and you will probably immediately feel you would like to sit down at the table. The charming National Trust stewards know how to stop that but they will let you in on the most intimate secrets of the high society in the early 19th century. You can ask any question you want and will always receive a precise and humorous answer. *Daily March, Nov 11am–3pm, April–June, Sept, Oct 10am–5pm, July, Aug 10am–7pm | entrance fee £6.50 | 7 Charlotte Square | www.nts.org.uk*

Elegant Edinburgh: Georgian façades in the New Town

4 NATIONAL GALLERY OF SCOTLAND & ROYAL SCOTTISH ACADEMY ●
(110 A2) (*ωι E4–5*)

These two temples to the arts designed by William Playfair before 1859 are second to none as Edinburgh's Neoclassicist highlights. The forest of Doric columns at the end of *The Mound* will probably make some tourists think of the famous description of Edinburgh as the 'Athens of the North'.

The art treasures in the *National Gallery of Scotland* cover the periods from the Middle Ages to Impressionism. There are paintings by Holbein, Titian and Rembrandt, as well as Gainsborough, Cézanne and van Gogh in the collection – the walls in the salons are full of pictures. INSIDER TIP Delicate watercolours by William Turner are displayed every January when the winter light can do them the least dam-

Art as far as the eye can see: a sea of pictures in the National Gallery of Scotland

age. The *Royal Scottish Academy* is used for special exhibitions.

A certain kind of cult has developed around the small portrait of *The Reverend Robert Walker Skating on Duddingston Loch*, painted by the high-society artist Henry Raeburn in 1795. It shows Walker, the vicar of Canongate Church and a member of the Honourable Edinburgh Skating Society on the ice, in a comically stiff pose balancing on one leg and wearing a forbidding black frock coat and top hat. Today, the picture seems to be something of a caricature of the society of the time and small copies of it on magnets really brighten up any fridge – so, don't miss out on a visit the shop! *Fri–Mon 10am–5pm, Thu 10am–7pm | free admission | The Mound | www.nationalgalleries.org | www.royalscottishacademy.org*

⑤ PRINCES STREET GARDENS ★ ●
(109–110 E–A 2–1) (*ⅉ D–F 5–4*)

The Gardens are Edinburgh's 'green lungs', the city's 'solarium' and a place where events are held. They were laid out when the New Town was being built and a long narrow lake, where supposedly witches and rubbish were disposed of, was drained. The park landscape that came into being stretches along the south side of the entire length of Princes Street, which was not built up on the park side so as not to obstruct the view of the skyline of the Old Town. The *East Gardens* are dominated by the Scott Monument and continue to *Waverley Station* – the main railway station named after a series of novels by Walter Scott – and the *Fruit Market Gallery*. By the way, the INSIDER TIP large clock on the tower of the palace-like

Balmoral Hotel is two minutes fast to prevent passengers from missing their trains. A train leaves Waverley every fifteen minutes for Glasgow and the charming little waiting room is also worth taking a look at. In December, a well-stocked Christmas Market is held behind the Scott Monument and an ice-skating rink is also opened. The *Dungeons* chamber of horrors *(Nov–Feb Mon–Fri 11am–4pm, Sat, Sun 10.30am–4.30pm, March–June and Sept, Oct daily 10am–5pm, July, Aug daily 10am–7pm | entrance fee £15 | 32 Market Street | www.thedungeons.com)* is a cavern full of combative figures; something for the intrepid with a fondness for trivial action. A steep street, *The Mound*, divides the park and leads up to the Old Town; on the way, the temple-like architecture of the *Royal Scottish Academy* and *National Gallery of Scotland* will possibly make you slow down a bit and stride past them ceremoniously. There is a INSIDER TIP relief at the foot of a flight of steps that provides a good 3-dimensional overview of Edinburgh's geography. The West Gardens are a wonderful place for a stroll, a climb up to the castle or for simply enjoying the view. This is also a very popular meeting place for local residents. In summer, the aroma of coffee wafts out of the *Open Air Café*, water bubbles in a fountain, floral arrangements add touches of colour and the fair-skinned Scots of the capital city attempt to get a bit of colour. The people of Edinburgh love their popular park on the slope and have a great time there throughout the year. This is the stage for the loudest music and festival events in the city and there is an especially festive atmosphere in the evening when one gazes up at the illuminated castle.

Things become a bit less profane and more picturesquely spooky at the West End. This is where *St Cuthbert Cemetery* connects with not one but two churches: *St Cuthbert's Kirk (5 Lothian Road | www.stcuthberts. net)* is a stately, roundish basilica in the midst of the green of the trees with an interior decorated in warm tones. *St John's (3 Lothian Road | www.stjohns-edinburgh. org.uk)* on the other hand is an overpowering Victorian barrage constructed in the late-Gothic Perpendicular style and decorated with the most exquisite church windows in town. Especially in winter, the gravestones in the cemetery provide a INSIDER TIP fabulous foreground for photos of the castle when there are no leaves on the trees to block the view.

RELAX & ENJOY

Enjoying spa-style activities is something rather new for the residents of the capital city but there are some exquisite feel-good locations in Edinburgh. The best is on the roof of the five-star ● *Sheraton Grand (spa daily from 8am, swimming from 6.30am | 3 hours £65 | 1 Festival Square, Lothian Road | www. onespa.com)*. It meets the highest international standards with a Turkish bath, aroma grottoes, massages, ergonomic beds, gym, showers that smell like you are in a rainforest, and a saltwater outdoor pool with a view of the city. The *Scotsman* boutique hotel and *Balmoral Grand Hotel* (both p. 79) also have new spa facilities that are not only open to hotel guests and, after your treatment, you can chat about what you have experienced in the bar or brasserie.

Unbelievably beautiful: the stained-glass works of art in St John's

6 ■ SCOTT MONUMENT ☼
(110 A1) (𝔐 E5)

Art is not only hidden inside the walls of the Scottish Gallery of Modern Art, the writer's monument to end all writer's monuments is located on Princes Street. After climbing up the 287 steps at several levels you will be able to look down on the city. In summer, there are long queues of people at the entrance waiting to get in and the narrow staircase means that some of them will still not have managed to get out again after an hour. In winter, on the other hand, it can happen that you will not be able to find the craftily inserted spiral staircase again after you have gone out onto one of the balconies unless somebody happens to be standing on it. When Walter Scott died in 1832, the decision was made to create a dramatic monument in his memory. There was a neo-Gothic spirit at this time of transition from the sober Georgian to the ostentatious Victorian style. This means that Scott was presented with a an ornate Gothic tower made of sandstone housing 64 figures from the writer's novels and 16 portrait busts of other Scottish poets. Today, the 200 ft high construction stands there like the spire of a church tower without a base. A quarry had to be reopened when renovation work was carried out in 1998/99 but the colour of the delicate sandstone has suffered – partly as a result of traffic pollution. *April–Sept daily 9am–7pm, Oct–March Mon–Sat 9am–3pm, Sun 10am–4pm | entrance fee £3.50 | East Prices Street Gardens*

■7 SCOTTISH NATIONAL PORTRAIT GALLERY (106 A5) (*Ø F4*)

This is where you can find the 'who's who' of Scottish society captured in every kind of portrait imaginable: an exhibition of Scottish heroes from Sean Connery or the author Irvine Welsh and football trainer Alex Ferguson to Bonnie Prince Charlie and – of course – Mary Stuart. After extensive renovations, the portrait museum was reopened in autumn 2011. *1 Queen Street | www.nationalgalleries.org*

MORE SIGHTS

Edinburgh exudes rural charm in Dean Village and Stockbridge to the west and northwest of the heart of the city.

The small river known as the Water of Leith creates a natural border between the elegant façades of the New Town and residential roads, hidden houses and suburban streets of shops such as *Raeburn Place*. Explore some of the small boutiques and rub shoulders with the locals at the bar. Linger for a while on the small bridges over the river and in front of carefully restored buildings from the industrial age in *Dean Village*. And if you have the stamina and the right shoes, follow the idyllic course of the river as far as Leith where the out-of-town port has developed into a place for gourmets and night-owls to enjoy themselves. If you keep going as far as the beach at *Portobello*, you will have completed an arc from the west to north-east around the centre of the capital city.

DEAN GALLERY ● (108 B1) (*Ø B4*)

There are two museums in Dean Village with its semi-rural atmosphere; this one is more intimate than the *Gallery of Modern Art* opposite. The exhibitions are dominated by Surrealism and Dadaism and there is also a replica of the studio where Eduardo Paolozzi (1924–2005), Edinburgh's greatest modern artist, once worked.

It is a good idea to start in Stockbridge and make the building from the 19th century the final destination of a short hike along the idyllic River Leith. The charming little café – always full of students and art aficionados – has a fascinating exhibition of photographs of Paolozzi. Once outside, you should not miss out on a visit to well cared-for, INSIDER**TIP** atmospheric *Dean Cemetery*. *Daily 10am–5pm | Belford Road Dean Village | www.nationalgalleries.org | bus 13*

INSIDER**TIP** PORTOBELLO (113 D1) (*Ø 0*)

Its claim to be the 'Brighton of the North' is definitely a bit exaggerated. But, the large sandy beach only about 30 minutes away from Princes Street is very popular on hot summer days. The long promenade, the typical, nostalgic Victorian seaside charm, cafés, pubs, ice cream and chips, and the curious middle-class houses in the streets behind the beach make an excursion here well worth it. In winter, it is the perfect place for a melancholic stroll along the seashore as far as the newly designed port district of Leith. *Buses 12, 15, 26, 32, 42, 49*

ROYAL BOTANIC GARDEN ★ (105 D–E 1–2) (*Ø C–D 1–2*)

Scotland is famous for its magnificent landscaped gardens and the Royal Botanic Garden is the epitome of floral glory. The complex is 200 years old, somewhat younger than London's Kew Gardens, but it is also an important research site. With its rock and Chinese gardens, pavilions and wonderful, recently renovated, glasshouses, it is the only tropical location in

Edinburgh. It also has the oldest collections of botanical literature in Great Britain. You will need some extra time to visit the shop and café terrace. The view of the medieval skyline of the city from the ❄ *Terrace Café* is a real delight (*May–Sept daily 9.30am–6 pm | tel. 0131 5 52 06 16 | Budget*). *Nov–Feb daily 10am–4pm, March, Oct 10am–6pm, April–Sept 10am–7pm | entrance fee: glasshouses £4.50, families £9; garden: free | Inverleith Row Stockbridge | www.rbge.org.uk | buses 8, 17, 23, 27*

ROYAL YACHT BRITANNIA ★ ●
(111 E1) (*∭ K1*)

Her Majesty set out to sea in this Art Deco yacht from 1953 to 1997; she visited and played hostess to illustrious statesmen, members of royal families and even Gandhi. The yacht is decorated in a style typical of the taste of post-war Britain – which some people from other countries find hard to get used to. The audio-guide will help you place certain figures in the right context. Visitors go on board the queen-sized yacht in the port of Leith through the *Ocean Terminal* (with its own shopping centre) planned by the star designer Terence Conran. *Jan–March, Nov, Dec daily 10am–3.30pm, April, May, June, Oct daily 10am–4pm, July–Sept 9.30am–4.30pm | entrance fee £12 | Ocean Drive | Leith | www.royalyachtbritannia.org.uk | buses 1, 11, 22, 34, 35, 36*

🞐 SCOTTISH NATIONAL GALLERY OF MODERN ART ★ (108 A2) (*∭ A5*)

What is possibly the best museum in town is located directly opposite the Dean Gallery – go inside, even though you might have had enough of Neoclassicist sandstone buildings. The international artistic universe of the past hundred years is represented here – from Matisse to Hockney and Pollock, alongside various modern Scottish art movements. The café is wonderful and is well worth a visit not only for its tasty snacks made with fresh local products – the same applies to Charles Jencks' landscape sculpture. And after all this culture, you can make your way back to town along the River Leith with a fresh spring in your step. *Daily 10am–5pm | Belford Road | www.national galleries.org | bus 13*

BOOKS & FILMS

▶ **Shallow Grave** – Danny Boyle's first film (1994) already had Ewan McGregor as its star. In the dark comedy, three young whipper-snappers from Edinburgh unexpectedly find a case full of drug money and a corpse they need to get rid of in a hurry.

▶ **Doors Open** – A thriller by Ian Rankin without the solitary Inspector Rebus about an ingenious painting robbery in Edinburgh.

▶ **Trainspotting** – Notoriously famous novel by Irvine Welsh that digs deep into the life of drug addicts in Leith. Welsh cut open Edinburgh's soul with his social scalpel and Danny Boyle filmed it masterfully in 1996.

▶ **Complicity** – A serial killer bumps people off one after the other in Edinburgh but, for some strange reason, the reader finds him almost likeable. A dark character study of the city by Iain Banks.

Art is not only hidden behind the walls of the Scottish Gallery of Modern Art

FURTHER AFIELD

GLASGOW (112 A1) (*🗺 0*)

Scotland's largest city with a population of 750,000 is only a fifty-minute train ride away from Waverley Station; there are four departures every hour. You will come across a glaring contrast to Edinburgh: post-industrial charm, a creative art and music scene, rough slang, no-frills urbanity. Glasgow is more hectic than Edinburgh and not all homogenous. The unsophisticated but hearty charm of the city appeals to many visitors. Unlike the more refined residents of Edinburgh, the Glaswegians don't mince their words.

As soon as you leave *Queen Street Station*, you will feel the tingling large-city atmosphere. One hundred years ago, Glasgow was superior to London in almost all fields. You will get an idea of this when you cross *George Square* from the railway station to the Renaissance-style town hall, the *City Chambers*; Carrara marble was used for its extravagant interior around 1890. On the corner, the renovated post-industrial *Merchant City* – a magnet for shoppers, full of boutiques, art galleries, bars and restaurants – pulsates with life. A visit to the marvellous *Art School (www.gsa.ac.uk)* designed by the Art Nouveau genius Charles Mackintosh is an absolute must. After you leave the railway station, stroll past the windows on Buchanan and Sauchiehall Streets to *Renfrew Street* where you can admire the main work of this jack-of-all-trades. It is well worth taking a guided tour of the School. Fifteen minutes away to the west, the University and *Kelvingrove Museum*, part of which were constructed in the pompous Gothic style preferred by the Victorians, rise out of the idyllic *Kelvingrove Park* with a small stream flowing through it. Has this made you hungry for more? Then it's off to Glasgow's best Indian restaurant *(Mother India | 28 Westminster Terrace | Budget)*.

FOOD & DRINK

Edinburgh's restaurants are booming! The Scots have always placed great value on their Angus beef, fish, scallops and oysters. In the past 10 or 15 years, a new creativity – mostly with its roots in France – has found its way into their preparation.

This revolution in the culinary art has really made itself felt in the pubs. Simple pub food, such as fish 'n' chips, lasagne and stew, have become much tastier. Gastro pubs have developed small, exquisite menus that have become just as important as the list of whiskies and different types of ale. They also use many local products such as pheasant and mussels and often mention where they come from.

The setting also plays a major role. Since the mid 1990s, restaurants have opened in interesting, old buildings in the Old and New Towns. The former port of Leith has blossomed into Scotland's culinary centre; three of the chefs working there have been awarded at least one Michelin star. Cafés – usually open from 9am to 5pm or 6pm – are shooting up like mushrooms. But, in spite of all the changes, the new chefs do not ignore the old rustic hits from the local kitchen such as porridge, black pudding and haggis – however, today they are seasoned with more sophistication. Asian restaurants and continental cuisine round off Edinburgh's culinary scene.

Photo: The Hub Café

Just fish and chips – you must be joking! Both pub food and haute cuisine have really improved in Edinburgh

Lunch is usually served from noon until 2pm and dinner from around 5pm to 11pm. Take-aways are open until 1am or 2 am, if you are still hungry. Restaurants and pubs now have a good selection of wines. Others, that do not have the necessary license, let you bring your own wine to accompany your meal; however, they charge a corkage fee *(BYOB – bring your own bottle, £1–3)*, others offer *BYOB* as an extra.

CAFÉS & CAFÉ RESTAURANTS

THE CHOCOLATE TREE ● ⏱
(109 D–E6) *(🛱 D8)*

It is worth travelling a long way to find such fantastic sweet goodies. This shop to the south of the Old Town offers chocolates made with ingredients from organic farms, cakes from Germany, and novel ideas such as absinthe masks and ginger Buddhas.

Man's best friend on the walls, delicious fish dishes on your plate: The Dogs

You can sample them at the small tables. The makers are at the *Farmers' Market* near the castle on Saturday. *Daily | 123 Bruntsfield Place | tel. 0131 228 3144*

CAFÉ TRUVA (111 D1) (*M H4*)

This is the place to try INSIDER TIP real oriental coffee and Turkish cuisine. The shop with the Mediterranean flair has tables outside under the arcades – a rare thing in Edinburgh. Turkish breakfast, a splendid selection of *meze* (starters), chocolates and *baklava*. *Daily | 231–251 Canongate, Royal Mile | Old Town | tel. 0131 556 95 24 | www.cafetruva.com*

HERBIE (105 E4) (*M D3*)

This café-cum-delicatessen in the western section of the New Town serves excellent coffee and delicious sandwiches. It's difficult to make a choice from all the special types of ham and dreamy chocolates. *Closed Sun | North West Circus Place | tel. 0131 226 72 12 | www.herbieofedinburgh. co.uk*

THE HUB CAFÉ (110 A2) (*M E5*)

This tower of a former neo-Gothic church is the 'Hub' everything on the upper section of the Royal Mile revolves around. You can buy tickets for the Edinburgh Festival here and it also has the best café terrace near the castle. *Daily | Castlehill, Royal Mile | Old Town | tel. 0131 4 73 20 67 | www. thehub-edinburgh.com*

SPOON (110 B2) (*M F5*)

The sober atmosphere of this daytime café is a contrast to the labyrinthine Old Town. Simple snacks including toasted sandwiches and delicious, finely-composed, soups. *Closed Sun | 6a Nicholson Street | Old Town | tel. 0131 5 56 69 22*

VALVONA & CROLLA ★

The Italian delicatessen café *(Budget)* with hams hanging from the ceiling, the aroma of coffee, cheese, pastries and freshly-baked bread in the air, is the result of a wave of Italian emigration more than 100 years ago. Enter the magical world of delicious breakfast and first-rate luncheon creations in the parent shop in Broughton or stop by the *Vin Caffè* with the upstairs restaurant *(Moderate)* for a glass of wine. *Delicatessen café: Mon–Sat 8am–6pm, Sun 10.30am–5pm | 19 Elm Row, Leith Walk | Broughton* (106 C4) *(ₘ G3)* | *tel. 0131 5 56 60 66; Restaurant Vin Caffè: Closed Sat/Sun | Multrees Walk, St Andrew Square | New Town* (106 A5) *(ₘ F4)* | *tel. 0131 5 57 00 88 | www.valvonacrolla.co.uk*

GASTRO-PUBS & BISTROS

THE DOGS (109 F1) *(ₘ E4)*

It is a rather strange feeling to have melancholy eyes staring down at you from an XXL print while you are eating. Or to find a book with quotations about dogs (from Franz Kafka and the like) on your way to the toilet. This is supposedly due to the fact that the owner of the gastro-pub only survived a depression because he had to take his dog out regularly for a walk. The menu lists hearty food from times when the Scots were not so well-off and even includes *faggots and rumbledethumps* (meat balls with baked potatoes and cabbage).

The concept of mixing old and new dishes, laid-back service and low prices is a success – branches have been opened next door: *Amore Dogs (daily | 104 Hanover Street | tel. 0131 2 20 51 55 | Budget)* serves pizza and Italian-Scottish dishes, *Sea Dogs (daily | 43 Rose Street | tel. 0131 2 25 80 28 | Moderate)* is devoted to fish. *Daily | 110 Hanover Street | New Town | tel. 0131 2 20 12 08*

KING'S WARK (111 F2) *(ₘ L2)*

In the 17th century, this dingy, tatty building was part of King James I's building complex. Leith has now become considerably finer and this well-known, popular pub restaurant has also been spruced up. The generous servings of *classic pub food* (the thickest chips in town) have, however, been remained; you can eat more sophisticated fare next door. *Daily | 36 The Shore | Leith | tel. 0131 5 54 92 60 | buses 1, 10, 16, 22, 35, 36*

SKIPPERS ★ (111 E2) *(ₘ L1)*

This small gastro-pub seems to be somewhat lost although it was already here about 30 years ago when Leith was only dock land. It has preserved its closeness to the sea and serves the best fish dishes in this price category. *Daily | 1a Dock Place | Leith | tel. 0131 5 54 10 18 | www.skippers.co.uk | buses 1, 10, 16, 22, 35*

★ **Valvona & Crolla**
Italian sensuality contrasts with the sober lines of the New Town → p. 52

★ **Skippers**
The finest fish dishes in an old building at the port → p. 53

★ **Urban Angel**
Edinburgh's most popular café-brasserie relies on organic products and fair trade → p. 54

★ **Atrium**
Some people say that this is Edinburgh's best restaurant → p. 54

★ **David Bann**
The best vegetarian restaurant is in the Old Town → p. 55

★ **The Grain Store**
Atmosphere and service are the fourth course of a splendid meal → p. 56

MARCO POLO HIGHLIGHTS

RESTAURANTS: EXPENSIVE

URBAN ANGEL ★ ☺
(109 F1) (*Ⅲ E4*)

This cheerful brasserie is especially popular with the locals. The tapas, fish, poultry and brownies are pure poetry. You enjoy your meal with a clear conscience because the head chef David Spanner follows the gastronomic trend and INSIDER**TIP** uses as many organic products as possible; most of them are fair trade. *Daily | 121 Hanover Street | New Town | tel. 0131 2 25 62 15 | www.urban-angel.co.uk*

RESTAURANTS: EXPENSIVE

ATRIUM ★ (109 E3) (*Ⅲ D5*)

Post-modern interior with warm colours. This restaurant in the foyer of the *Traverse Theatre* was in part responsible for the start of Edinburgh's wave of fine dining in the 1990s; it has since been renovated and many insiders still consider it the best restaurant in town. It serves fusion-cooking without any frills and also caters for vegetarians. There are INSIDER**TIP** less expensive off-season set meals on the website. *Closed Sat lunch and Sun | 10 Cambridge Street | Old Town | tel. 0131 2 28 88 82 | www.atriumrestaurant.co.uk*

HOTEL DU VIN BISTRO
(110 B3) (*Ⅲ F6*)

A good tip – and that not only because of its relaxed but sophisticated atmosphere. The restaurant is spacious but manages to remain intimate and the modern, no-nonsense inner courtyard in the old, listed building is a rare thing to find in Edinburgh. The kitchen serves European food and delicious creations for vegetarians. The INSIDER**TIP** petits fours that taste like berry-marshmallows, Turkish delight or Irn-Bru, Scotland's national soft drink, are delightful. *Daily | 11 Bristo Place | Old Town | tel. 0131 2 47 49 00 | www.hotel duvin.com*

THE KITCHIN (111 E2) (*Ⅲ L1*)

The industrial grey tones of the interior of Tom Kitchin's gourmet address create a

GOURMET RESTAURANTS

Martin Wishart (111 F2) (*Ⅲ L2*)

The local, but widely-travelled chef has managed to keep his Michelin star since 2001 and his pleasantly no-nonsense restaurant in Leith is considered by many to have the best cooking in Edinburgh if not in all of Scotland. That is not only a matter of taste: Wishart creates extremely sophisticated culinary delights out of exclusively Scottish products such as beef, oysters, game, fish and vegetables of the season. The service is just as outstanding as the European cuisine. *Set meals from £60 | closed Sun, Mon | 54 The Shore | Leith | tel. 0131 5 53 35 57 |* *www.martin-wishart.co.uk | bus 1, 10, 16, 22, 35, 36*

The Witchery & Secret Garden
(109 F2) (*Ⅲ E5*)

Absolutely in keeping with its location in the finest part of the Old Town, this two-storey restaurant in a building from the 16th century attracts guests with its castle-like elegance. You can get dressed up to eat here, but it is not essential. The food is really excellent. *Set meals from £35 | daily | Castlehill, Royal Mile | Old Town | tel. 0131 2 25 56 13 | www. thewitchery.com*

Exquisite, award-winning cuisine is served in the reduced industrial atmosphere of The Kitchin

feeling for the past history of this former whisky toll house. After two months in Leith, this Edinburgh chef was awarded his second Michelin star; he serves all that Scotland has to offer coupled with French refinement. Sea urchins, rabbit or beef – this is how straightforwardly the dishes are listed on the menu *(Expensive)*. *Closed Sun, Mon | 78 Commercial Quay | Leith | tel. 0131 55 17 55 | www.thekitchin.com | buses 1, 10, 16, 22, 35*

PLUMED HORSE
(111 E2) *(𝄢 L2)*

An address typical of the new gourmet district in Leith: Tony Borthwick's restaurant with a Michelin star is almost hidden in the former port area. The restrained interior in bright, creamy tones takes second place to the exquisite, expensive dishes – French creations from Scotland's meadows and rivers. *Closed Sun, Mon | 50–54 Henderson Street | Leith | tel. 0131 54 55 56 | www.plumedhorse.co.uk | buses 1, 10, 16, 22, 36*

RESTAURANTS: MODERATE

DAVID BANN ★ ☺ (110 C2) *(𝄢 G5)*

It is hard to imagine Scottish cooking without meat and that is what makes this excellent vegetarian restaurant in the lower Old Town so special. The risottos, *galettes, polentas* and homemade ravioli are delicious and can even convince meat-eaters to sample vegetarian fare. Vegans will also find what they are looking for here. You should also try the INSIDERTIP Kelpie Ale brewed from seaweed. *Daily | 56–58 St Mary's Street | Old Town | tel. 0131 5 56 58 88 | www.davidbann.com*

DUBH PRAIS (110 B2) *(𝄢 F5)*

Small, low-ceilinged and without windows: typical of the Royal Mile. The exquisite cooking with Scottish products and the pleasantly small menu are almost unexpected in this tourist location – and a real delight. Haggis is served as a starter and there is Scottish cheese for dessert. *Closed Sun, Mon | 123b High Street, Royal Mile |*

LOCAL SPECIALITIES

▶ **Black pudding** – the famous blood and oat sausage comes from Stornoway

▶ **Brodick blue** – ewe's milk cheese from the Island of Arran

▶ **Caboc** – Highland soft-cheese in oatmeal

▶ **Cock-a-leekie** – chicken soup with leek and prunes

▶ **Cranachan** – full-fat whipped cream with toasted oatmeal, honey and whisky, served with raspberries

▶ **Crowdie** – fresh cheese from the Highlands

▶ **Cullen skink** – haddock soup with milk, potatoes and onions

▶ **Haggis** – sheep's stomach stuffed with heart, liver, lungs and oatmeal (photo above left)

▶ **Irn-Bru** – Scottish-made orange-coloured soft drink with caffeine, the success of which is a sore point with international companies – so far, takeover attempts have failed

▶ **Kail** – kale

▶ **Kippers** – salted, smoked herrings

▶ **Oysters** – those from Loch Fyne are the best

▶ **Poached smoked haddock** – served with poached eggs

▶ **Skirlie** – oatmeal groats served with onions

▶ **Stovies** – stewed beef with onions (leftover stew – photo above right)

Old Town | tel. 0131 5 57 57 32 | www. dubhpraisrestaurant

THE GRAIN STORE ★ ●
(110 A2) (*ØØ E5*)

If Michelin stars were awarded for atmosphere, as well as cool but attentive service, The Grain Store would be a candidate. Moderate prices for lunch and dinner by candlelight with bare vaulted walls: the Old Town without the kitsch. The kitchen even turns something as substantial as *black pudding* into a delicacy. Scottish pheasant and oysters accompanied by interesting salads and sinful desserts – everything is as it should be. *Closed Sun lunch | 20 Victoria Street | Old Town | tel. 0131 2 25 76 35 | www.grainstore-restaurant.co.uk*

TANG'S (110 A3) (*ØØ F6*)

There are no frills in this Japanese restaurant. Guests are served cod in *miso* sauce on a bamboo leaf or delicious *bento* lunches, all finished off with a Japanese dessert and the aroma of lemongrass and jasmine. *Closed Mon | 44 Candlemaker Row | Old Town | tel. 0131 2 20 50 00*

RESTAURANTS: BUDGET

BARIOJA (110 B2) *(𝄞 G5)*

You will find this tapas bar with its Spanish staff and wine list in the Old Town. Unfortunately, the tapas are not on display at the bar for you to choose but they are still authentic. There are not many tables on the ground floor and you will probably have to sit in the basement if you have not reserved. During the day, Barioja is good place to have a glass of wine and recover from all the sightseeing. The set meal at lunchtime consists of four tapas. The Spanish restaurant next door *(Expensive)* is run by the same owners. *Daily | 15–19 Jeffrey Street | Old Town | tel. 0131 5 57 36 22 | www.barioja.co.uk*

KEBAB MAHAL (110 B3) *(𝄞 G6)*

Curries, *biryanis* and the like are not expensive and absolutely delicious in this fashionable Indian restaurant. This is the right place for people looking for a relaxed, cosmopolitan dinner and an evening with a colourful cross section of Edinburgh's population. And, if you feel hungry late at night, food is served until midnight and even later at the weekend. *Daily | 7 Nicholson Square | Old Town | tel. 0131 6 67 52 14 | www.kebab-mahal.co.uk*

OLIVE BRANCH (106 B4) *(𝄞 F3)*

This café-restaurant with its post-industrial design is one of the most popular in the fashionable Broughton district. You sit very close to your neighbours and can take in the fascinating mix of guests and also see what is going on outside on the street – thanks to the large windows. The servings of roast and fried food are extremely generous. Popular place for

Great for people watching: Olive Branch

Sunday brunch. *Daily | 2 Broughton Place | New Town | tel. 0131 5 57 85 89 | www. theolivebranchscotland.co.uk*

LOW BUDGET

▶ A glass of wine with a main course for £12 is called *Simply du Vin* in the exquisite bistro of the *Hotel du Vin (p. 54)*.

▶ There are some fish and chip shops that will make sure that you don't starve after midnight – large servings, often until 2am. *The Deep Sea* opposite the Playhouse Theatre on Calton Hill is one of the best.

▶ The service-industry capital of Scotland has become a good address for eating inexpensively at lunchtime; you can find two-course set meals from £13. There is an especially wide choice around Grassmarket and in Broughton. The top restaurant *The Witchery (p. 54)* also offers two-course pre or post-theatre meals for £15.

SHOPPING

WHERE TO START?

CITY You should begin on the **Royal Mile (110–111 A–D 2–1)** (*M E–H 4–5)*. You will find real Scottish couture if you turn right onto Victoria Street where Armstrong's second-hand shop lies waiting between the two independent Totty Rocks and Fabhatrix boutiques. Tartan to keep your ears warm can be found on Candlemaker Row. Multrees Walk is full of international haute couture. Don't miss good old Jenners on Princes Street!

An increasing number of top British and international brands have found their way to Edinburgh since it was upgraded to the real capital city of Scotland.

Princes Street is the place to go if you are looking for department stores and book and electronics shops. Things are a bit more fashionable on the parallel *George Street* and reach their peak on exclusive *St Andrew Square* and *Multrees Walk. The Royal Mile* is in the grip of tartans, oatmeal biscuits and bottles of whisky, but *Grassmarket* and the neighbouring streets are full of charming little boutiques selling fashions and accessories made in Scotland *(www.grassmarket.net)*. You

Photo: Jenners department store

Design made in Scotland, chic fashions, imaginative second-hand shops and everything for the whisky connoisseur – start your spree here!

should definitely not miss out on the more individual and off-beat designer shops in the gay district around *Broughton Street* or INSIDER TIP▶ the wide range of shops in the well-off *Bruntsfield* area around 20 minutes on foot from Princes Street. Most shops are open from 9am to 6pm from Monday to Saturday, often until 8pm on Thursday, and from 11am to 5pm on Sunday.

BOOKS & MUSIC

COCKBURN STREET (110 A–B2) (*🗺 F5*)
Cockburn Street attracts fans who are not only interested in mainstream music. *Underground Solu'shn (no. 9)* is the top address for records for DJs. *Avalanche (no. 63)* offers independent CDs and second-hand records. *Fopp* is an independent music warehouse and also has a branch in the

Cheese, cheese and more cheese: not only gourmets will sing the praises of I. J. Mellis

New Town *(7 Rose Street)*. The music shops are the INSIDERTIP best places to get information and buy tickets for live acts.

WATERSTONE'S (109 E2) *(ﾉﾉ D5)*

There is a special Edinburgh section in each of the bookshop chain's branches. They also offer a fine opportunity for those interested in literature to stock up on the INSIDERTIP works of Rankin, Welsh and Burns. A typical service: handwritten reviews by the staff are displayed. Open until 7pm on Sunday. *Branches 3–14 and 128–128a Princes Street, 83 George Street | www.waterstones.com*

DELICATESSEN

CROMBIES (106 B4) *(ﾉﾉ F3)*

An exquisite butcher's with game and pork 'designer sausages' refined with mango, port and blue cheese. This is also the place to buy haggis for your picnic or to take home with you. *97–101 Broughton Street*

I. J. MELLIS (110 A2) *(ﾉﾉ E5)*

Mellis has catered to the residents of the capital since 1993 and now has three cheese shops. Visitors will discover what the Scots are capable of making out of milk: excellent *bries, cheddars* and blue cheeses. You can taste *Clava Brie, Caboc, Connage Crowdie, Isle of Mull Cheddar* and the – often overpowering – *Lanark Blue* in the shop. There is also an exquisite selection of Continental cheeses. Stock up on INSIDERTIP cheese for your picnic in Princes Street Gardens or for your stroll along the Water of Leith. *30a Victoria Street | Old Town; 6 Bakers Place is also easy to reach | Stockbridge*

DEPARTMENT STORES

HARVEY NICHOLS ★ (110 A1) *(ﾉﾉ F4)*

The building of the most exclusive British department store on aristocratic St Andrew Square is unassuming compared with the luxurious goods hanging from the pegs and on the shelves inside. Shirts from Alexander McQueen from £180, suits made by the most famous Saville Row tailor, Gieves & Hawkes, as well as the usual international brands. There is a large restaurant with a view of the square on the upper floor. The selection of whiskies, rums and other drinks in front of it will make connoisseurs go weak at the knees: a bottle of 1964 Bowmore for a little over £2800, a 1974 Ardbeg for a good £460 or an old Havana Club at £1200. *30–34 St Andrew Square | www.harvey nichols.com*

JENNERS ● (110 A1) (*∅ F4*)

Jenners' Victorian façade is especially striking; it has occupied the corner of Princes Street since 1834. But its reputation as 'the Harrods of the North' is only partly justified. Jenners is a confusing labyrinth of around 100 departments and is unique in the world of renowned department stores partly because of this. But that is exactly why you should pop in and admire the high-ceilinged grand hall before getting lost. You will meet half of Edinburgh – usually the more moneyed half – during your expedition and they will probably look just as confused as you. The lifts travel at a snail's pace, the escalators are well-hidden; in a word, Jenners is the perfect place to get out of the rain. You can buy almost anything there although the emphasis is on clothing and material. In the meantime, Jenners has introduced an increasing number of new brands; probably as a result of the competition from Harvey Nichols. *48 Princes Street | www. houseoffraser.co.uk*

MARKETS & WINDOW SHOPPING

BRUNTSFIELD PLACE
(109 D–E6) (*∅ D8*)

Would you like to spend a couple of hours in a nearby suburb with charming cafés, bakeries and more than a dozen fascinating souvenir shops without any of the usual Scottish kitsch? Bruntsfield is only a twenty-minute walk from the Royal Mile

---

MARCO POLO HIGHLIGHTS

★ **Harvey Nichols**
Department store for lovers of brand names and an expensive taste → p. 60

★ **21st Century Kilts**
Extraordinary items for real men → p. 62

★ **Armstrong's**
Second-hand, but still in fashion: garments with an illustrious past → p. 62

★ **Joey D**
Handbags and more for individualists → p. 63

★ **George Street**
Edinburgh's aristocratic address is the perfect location for traditional, high-quality boutiques → p. 63

★ **Sheila Fleet Jewellery**
Art from the Orkney Islands: sublime interpretations of the Scottish landscape turned into jewellery → p. 64

★ **Royal Mile Whiskies**
Not only connoisseurs will feel they are in paradise: there can't be any greater choice of whisky and whiskey than here → p. 65

and is also easy to reach by bus. There are boutiques selling wooden toys, jewellery, novel wallpaper, shoes and children's clothing – the selection is first-rate. *Buses 11, 15, 16, 17, 23, 45*

FARMER'S MARKET ● (109 E3) (*ΩΩ D5*)

The weekly speciality market at the castle is the first place you should visit on Saturday. There is nothing else like it in Edinburgh and you will get a good overview of all the fish, cheese, pickles and vegetables that can be bought there. If you have not had breakfast, you can even start the day here with take-away porridge. *9am–2pm | Castle Terrace*

INSIDER TIP RAEBURN PLACE
(104–105 C–D3) (*ΩΩ B–C3*)

There is row of shops next to each other along the main street in Stockbridge (to the west of the Water of Leith). This is where the locals buy their fish, second-hand books, tea and go to the hairdresser. The street will almost make you feel you are in a village; there is a lot to see in the shops and pubs and you will find some real bargains – how about Dickens' *Oliver Twist* complete with a bookmark for next to nothing. *Stockbridge*

FASHION

21ST CENTURY KILTS ★
(109 F1) (*ΩΩ E4*)

Men who wear kilts pose a genuine threat to female fashion domination. The kilts made by Howie Nicholsby give men plenty of room to stretch their legs and appear traditional and avant-garde at the same time. They can be worn with Crocs, shoes or parachutist's boots. Shoes with low heels make these kilts of wool, leather or even PVC real eye-catchers – that's presumably what metrosexuality is all about. *48 Thistle Street | www.21stcenturykilts.co.uk*

ANTA (110 A3) (*ΩΩ E5*)

Two small shops only a stone's throw from each other. Once you pass through the door, you will find it hard not to become infected by tartan fever. Annie Stewart uses the gentle colours of Scotland's Highlands and coasts in her exquisite woollen blankets, carpets, handbags, suitcases and even porcelain. Tartan without the kitsch! *93 West Bow | 73 Grassmarket | www.anta.co.uk*

ARMSTRONG'S ★ (110 A3) (*ΩΩ E5*)

This second-hand shop now has cult character. Kylie Minogue and the Franz Ferdinand Band have rummaged around here looking for clothes from the good old Victorian and Georgian periods that are still in perfect condition. Of course, there is not only Brit-retro but also *tweed* and *kilts* (from £110) not to forget the *sporran* – the pouch worn with a kilt (from £40). *83 Grassmarket | www.armstrong vintage.co.uk*

BILL BABER (110 A3) (*ΩΩ E5*)

The knitwear designer describes the personal style of his personal label as a cross between handcraft and fashion. Linen in particular, but also cotton and silk are used in the production of pullovers and jackets that all takes place in a back room. *66 Grassmarket | www.billbaber.com*

CORNICHE (110 B2) (*ΩΩ G5*)

Unpretentious boutique with intriguing if expensive individual items – although sometimes good bargains can be had, too. Worth a visit just to see Vivienne Westwood's creations. In addition, playful 'kilt-like' trousers for men. *2 Jeffrey Street | www.corniche.org.uk*

INSIDER TIP FABHATRIX
(110 A3) (*ΩΩ F5*)

Sherlock Holmes deerstalker hats made of Harris Tweed for the men, wispy fascinators for the women, and every conceivable kind of felt, woollen or silk, hand-made headwear. Fawns Reid is the most sought-after milliner in Edinburgh. *13 Cowgate | www.fabhatrix.com*

GEORGE STREET ★
(109 E–F1) *(🌐 D–E4)*

The most aristocratic axis through the New Town is the place to look for classic fashion. It invites visitors to take a stroll

JOEY D ★ (106 A–B4) *(🌐 F3)*

Unique items for men and women made of recycled material. The designer Joey D even made Elton John chic! The most outlandish appliqués and vivid prints, but always wearable. Clothes are first cut up and then reassembled to form new creations. **INSIDER TIP** The handbags are the most unconventional articles. Creative, urban, sexy – and, of course with a bit of tartan. *54 Broughton Street | www.joey-d.co.uk*

Recycling material for hip fashion lovers in the capital by the designer Joey D

past the clothes shops – most of them British and famous throughout the world. You will find respected outfitters' including Jack Wills who provides British yuppies with their clothes, Church's, the time-honoured shoemakers, Laura Ashley, Karen Miller and Jigsaw for ladies, Moss for the man in his elegant suit, as well as the classic shirt-maker T.M. Lewin and the American Brooks Brothers. Many shops are open until 5pm on Sunday. *www.edinburgh georgestreet.co.uk*

MULTREES WALK (110 A1) *(🌐 F4)*

This small street in the New Town has developed into the right place to buy top international brands such as Armani, Louis Vuitton and Mulberry. *St Andrew Square*

THE ROYAL MILE (110 B2) *(🌐 G5)*

Women should definitely look into this shop with its **INSIDER TIP** gossamer-fine stocking creations with various tartan patterns. *11 High Street, Royal Mile | www. tartantights.com*

JEWELLERY

TOTTY ROCKS (110 A2) (*M E5*)

INSIDER TIP Outstanding, small independent fashion label. Unique clothes, handbags and jewellery are designed in the rooms above the little shop. The two young designers, Holly Mitchell and Lynsey Blackburn, are among the top girls in the young Scottish fashion business and now teach at the Edinburgh School of Art. *40 Victoria Street | www.tottyrocks.com*

JEWELLERY

ROCK CANDY
(109 E1) (*M D-E4*)

This small shop away from the main streets of the New Town is a treasure trove full of modern, charming jewellery. Steel, titanium, gold and silver are woven together to create modern rings. There are also fabulous cufflinks for men. *111 Rose Street | New Town | www.rockcandygallery.com*

SHEILA FLEET JEWELLERY ★
(105 D4) (*M D3*)

The jewellery designer has let the magical flair of her home on the Orkney Islands flow into her creations. For example, in her 'Rowan Collection' Sheila Fleet adapts details of the Scottish landscape and the reflection of the moon on the sea to create a delicate interpretation of the Highland rowan in jewellery. The changing tide, pebbles rounded by the sea and the colours at the edge of pools of water at low tide can be felt in her pieces and make it difficult to resist buying them. *18 St Stephen Street | Stockbridge*

TRADITIONAL SCOTTISH

BAGPIPES GALORE (111 D1) (*M H4*)

Do you really want to buy a bagpipe? Then this is the right place for you no matter whether you are a professional, beginner, souvenir hunter or not quite sure – and are therefore interested in getting your hands on a INSIDER TIP used instrument. *82 Canongate*

HAWICK CASHMERE
(110 A3) (*M E5*)

The lightweight, expensive goats' wool comes from China and Mongolia but it has been processed in the small town of Hawick in the south of Scotland since 1874. Luxury knitwear brand whose traditional goods are famous worldwide. *71–81 Grassmarket | www.hawickcashmere.com*

JUST SCOTTISH
(110 A2) (*M F5*)

There are countless shops selling shoddy Scottish souvenirs in the Old Town but this one will surprise you with the high quality of its goods. No matter whether you are looking for oatmeal biscuits or tartan things, you will find them here. *4–6 North Bank Street*

KINLOCH ANDERSON (111 E2) *(🛍 L1)*
Highland dress *at its best* has been sold here since 1868. This is a serious kilt shop for connoisseurs and those who want to become one. A small museum gives information on the history of the various clans' tartans. *4 Dock Street | Leith*

ROYAL MILE WHISKIES ⭐
(110 A2) *(🛍 F5)*
It is said that the shop has more than 300 kinds of whisky in stock and you are welcome to taste them. However, it makes

by Joyce Forsyth will make you forget it. Knitwear to clothe the lady with a taste for unusual patterns from head to toe. *42 Candlemaker Row*

SCOTTISH WHISKY HERITAGE CENTRE
(109 F2) *(🛍 E5)*
A tour through the history of whisky will put you in the right mood to buy a bottle or two of the almost 280 kinds on sale here. The shop near the castle also sees whisky as a form of entertainment. *354 Castlehill, Royal Mile*

Don't even try to count them: there are more than 300 kinds of whisky at Royal Mile Whiskies

more sense to be completely sober and let the imaginative labels and names inspire you when you make your choice. *379 High Street, Royal Mile*

SCOTTISH DESIGNER KNITWEAR
(110 A3) *(🛍 F5–6)*
This canyon of a street in the Old Town might appear rather gloomy but the colours and vivacity of the fashions designed

WHISKY SHOP (110 A2) *(🛍 E5)*
A small, pleasant independent whisky shop stacked to the ceiling with malts including varieties from the new distilleries on Shetland *(Black Wood)* and Islay *(Kilcommin)*. A tip for present hunters: the 200 and 500 ml bottles of ▐INSIDER🔖▶ whisky filled directly from the barrel are sure to delight whisky-lovers at home. *28 Victoria Street | www.whiskyshop.com*

ENTERTAINMENT

CITY WHERE TO START?

A cocktail in the **Dragonfly (109 F3)** *(🗺 E6)* is a good place to start. The exuberant nightlife of the Old Town is just a few yards away, between Grassmarket and Cowgate. Fans of the more fashionable New Town style navigate towards the area between St Andrew and George Square. Homosexuals will be drawn towards Broughton. Lovers of good jazz will head for the Jazz Bar before moving on to the Royal Oak for a midnight folk jam session.

Edinburgh also shows what it is capable of at night. The action starts in the small clubs, cinemas or in one of the countless pubs. The atmosphere in Edinburgh is more lounge-like than loud, more folk and jazz than rock.

The evening usually gets underway in a pub. The trend is now away from the fish-'n'-chips variety towards the gastro-pub with a smaller, more sophisticated menu. This is usually accompanied by top-fermented ale rather than a glass of wine. If this is what you are looking for, the area between Raeburn Place and Circus Place in *Stockbridge* will meet your requirements. At the busy *Tollcross* corner the ladies' skirts

Edinburgh's nightlife is not wild as such. The town's old vaulted cellars are often crowded and full of music lovers

are shorter and their heels higher but this is also where you will find the best theatre. *George Street* has the reputation of being 'posh' and this makes the queues in front of the clubs longer. The cellars in the Old Town are often very crowded. Since the architect Terence Conran completed the *Ocean Terminal* with its restaurant in 2001, ★ *Leith* has developed into a popular place to go out and have fun in the evening.

THE BAILIE (105 D4) (*ĐĐ D3*)

The bar counter turns a full 360 degrees and there are probably at least the same number of drinks served here. With its cosy location in a cellar, the pub attracts students, bankers and sport-TV fans. In keeping with the trendy area near the bridge over the Leith, it serves good bar

Brauhaus is a paradise for beer fans

food (*Budget*). *Daily 11am–midnight | 2–4 St Stephen Street*

INSIDER TIP THE BANSHEE LABYRINTH
(110 B2) (*ω F5*)

The labyrinthine subterranean Banshee has three bar areas, seven crypt-like rooms, jukeboxes, a dance floor complete with pole and a small non-stop cinema showing horror films. Excellent DJ mix or live gigs: there are even cosy corners for a 'candlelight burger'. The 'shocking' action starts around 10pm and then you will soon lose any sense of time. *Daily | 29–35 Niddry Street*

BENNET'S (109 E5) (*ω D7*)
Wonderful Victorian décor including separées for women that were fashion-

able at the time; all of this with plenty of brass, wood and a large colourful window (this also makes it a good place to visit during the day). It is next to the *King's Theatre* and this means that the long bar is packed after performances. Theatre audiences apparently also like live rugby. A good place for people watching. *Sun–Wed 11am–11.30pm, Thu–Sat 11am–1pm | 8 Leven Street*

INSIDER TIP BRAUHAUS
(109 E4) (*ω D6*)

A popular small beer bar. You should make sure that you still have your wits about you when you go in so that you can make the right selection from the 360 different kinds of beer served. As the night progresses, the friendly barman will take care of that for you. Don't forget to have something to eat while you are trying the brew – maybe a pretzel? Young crowd, students and civilised football fans (TV). *Daily noon–1am | 105–107 Lauriston Place*

CAFÉ ROYAL CIRCLE BAR ★
(110 A1) (*ω F4*)

This is probably the most magnificent bar in town with its listed Victorian furnishings. The bar forms an island beneath a fascinating ceiling, the walls are decorated with tile paintings from 1886 showing prominent inventors – Benjamin Franklin, Isaac Newton, Michael Faraday, James Watt, etc. – looking down on the crowd of locals and gaping tourists. It is well-hidden close to the eastern end of Princes Street. The *Guildford Arms* at *1–5* on the same street is rather similar. *Mon–Wed 11am–11pm, Thu to midnight, Fri, Sat to 1am, Sun 12.30–11pm | 17 West Register Street*

DALRIADA (113 D1) (*ω 0*)
After a long stroll along the beach at Portobello, you can spend the early evening in this pub with a view of the sand and

sea. Burgers and sandwiches are served at lunchtime; there is music at the weekend. *Daily 11am–11pm, lunch noon–3pm | 77 The Promenade Portobello | buses 12, 15, 32, 42, 49*

THE DOME (106 A5) (*m E4*)

This ex-bank looks a bit like a temple with its pompous façade on chic George Street and a rear entrance with a garden terrace onto bustling Rose Street. 'Posh' locals meets here under the chandeliers hanging from the 50 ft-high ceilings for their *latte*, lunch or dinner. Overwhelmingly *chic!* *Daily | 14 George Street*

INSIDER TIP HALFWAY HOUSE

(110 B2) (*m F5*)

The Halfway House is a hidden meeting place for the locals. The smallest pub in Edinburgh is located on the landing of one of the typical steep streets of steps between the Royal Mile and Waverley Station. But, there is still enough room for four ale taps at the bar and 30 different malts behind it. The meals that come out of the tiny kitchen are solid hits: pheasant soup, wild boar sausages with mashed potatoes or typical Scottish *cullen skink* (smoked fish soup) are all freshly prepared using ingredients from Scottish enterprises

(Budget). Daily from 11am | 24 Fleshmarket Close

HECTORS (105 D3–4) (*m C3*)

Popular bar with candlelight, cosy corners and the latest music – with DJs at the weekend – that draws in Edinburgh's well-heeled, middle-class crowd. This is where the people of Edinburgh come out of their shell and it becomes easy to strike up a conversation. Often full and very lively. *Daily 9am–1am | 47–49 Deanhaugh Street and corner Raeburn Place*

INSIDER TIP JEKYLL AND HYDE

(109 F1) (*m E4*)

Terrifying design and Gothic atmosphere where cocktails named after the seven mortal sins are served. If you're with the right crowd, you can have an unforgettable evening in this labyrinthine, outlandishly kitschy pub. *Daily noon–1am | 112 Hanover Street*

A ROOM IN LEITH

(111 E–F 1–2) (*m L1*)

A balmy summer evening and nowhere to go? Take the bus to Leith and sit down with a bottle of wine you have brought with you (corkage £2.25, house wine £14) at one of the tables on the pontoon deck

---

★ **Leith**
The old port has become the most popular place to go out and have a good time → p. 67

★ **Café Royal Circle Bar**
Perfectly-tapped beer and extravagant Victorian elegance → p. 68

★ **Cabaret Voltaire**
First-rate music cellar with dance club; the best of its kind → p. 72

★ **The Voodoo Rooms**
Magnificently flamboyant event and cocktail bar for steamy nights → p. 71

★ **Sandy Bell's**
Daily folk-music sessions with local and international stars → p. 72

★ **Festival Theatre**
Edinburgh's top theatre for plays, opera and dance → p. 72

MARCO POLO HIGHLIGHTS

at the port behind one of the pleasant, up-scale pub restaurants. *The Pre-Theatre Dinner (Sun–Thu 5.30pm–6pm | Moderate)* is the most economical option. The building is a bit difficult to find; it is one of the remnants of the former customs and ferry port. *Daily noon–midnight | 1c Dock Place | | buses 1, 11, 22, 34, 35, 36*

INSIDER TIP SHEEP HEID INN
(113 D2) (*ↂ L7*)

The oldest pub in Scotland (1360) has welcomed countless guests and is now famous for its tasty food (Sunday lunch!). You have to walk for almost 4 miles from Holyroodhouse along the volcanic cliffs of Salisbury Crag beneath Arthur's Seat to reach this cosy inn. The pub not only provides fine views of the bizarre mountainous landscape, the Old Town and Parliament but also of Duddingston Loch (see p. 87). *Daily until 11pm | 43–45 The Causeway | bus 42*

THE STOCKBRIDGE TAP
(105 D3–4) (*ↂ C3*)

With its light wood, parquet floors without carpets and cheerful neighbourhood atmosphere, this pub in the centre of Stockbridge is absolutely un-Victorian. Six draft ales, any number of different kinds of whisky and a small menu with substantial British food, including a delicious pheasant casserole (*Budget*). *Daily 10am– midnight | corner Raeburn Place/St Bernhard's Row*

UNDERDOGS ● (105 F5) (*ↂ E4*)

Nightlife in the cellars of the New Town is usually not quite as spooky as in the Old Town – there is more of a lounge-like feeling. The drinks in the living-room atmosphere of the club are fairly inexpensive and nowhere near as bizarre and sinful as in Jeckyll & Hyde a few doors away. *Daily | 104 Hanover Street*

CLUBS

DRAGONFLY (109 F3) (*ↂ E6*)

The best cocktail bar in the Old Town. Everybody here is well dressed but not quite as super-stylishly as in the Opal Lounge. One of the cocktails is called 'Edinburgh Rocks', the setting is lounge-like and agreeably cool, the style somewhere between colonial and the 1970s. Snacks and tapas until 10pm. Reservation recommended. *52 West Port | tel. 0131 2 28 45 43 | www.dragonflycocktailbar.com*

OPAL LOUNGE (109 F1) (*ↂ E4*)

This bar is typical of the superior George Street scene in the wealthy New Town. The furnishings as well as the clothes of the late-night clubbers are very stylish. You can savour the Asian dishes or sip a cocktail or two. You should take a partner with you; it is difficult to make contact here. It is especially popular and trendy after 10pm – the queues waiting to get in show that. Informative homepage. *Sun–Fri 5pm–*

The Voodoo Rooms are a great location to while the night away in Edinburgh

3am Sat noon–3am, food to 10pm | admission after 10pm from £5.50 | 51a George Street | www.opallounge.co.uk

THE VOODOO ROOMS ⭐
(110 A1) (*𝄐 F4*)

The most popular lounge and cocktail bar in Edinburgh's nightlife scene is located directly above the most beautiful pub in the New Town, the Café Royal. The bombastic Victorian era style was revitalised and the cocktails brought excitingly up to date. This is not only a place for looks and drinks but for intimate band and cabaret performances. Superb, elegant chillout areas in all the bars and salons. *Sun–Thu 2pm–1am, Fri, Sat noon–3am | entrance fee from £4.50 | West Register Street 19a | www.thevoodoorooms.com*

CINEMAS

Although the people of Edinburgh like going to the cinema and the city would provide a great setting for films, comparatively few are made here. Most of the cult film *Trainspotting* was actually shot in Glasgow. You can find out what's showing in the daily newspapers.

FILMHOUSE (109 E3) (*𝄐 D6*)

The *Edinburgh Film Festival* is held in mid-June in the most interesting cinema, from the artistic point of view, in the city. The Filmhouse concentrates on classic films and relatively unknown features, as well as subtitled foreign-language films. Three screens. *Admission from £5 | Lothian Road*

INSIDER TIP ▶ SCOTSMAN SCREENING ROOM (110 B1) (*𝄐 F4*)

An insiders' tip with 46 leather armchairs, a 100 ft² screen and ice cream included in the admission price. Unfortunately, you can only enjoy the intimate atmosphere in the exclusive Scotsman Hotel on Sundays *(8pm)* and you should be sure to book in advance on the Internet. *Scotsman Hotel | admission £10 | 20 North Bridge | tel. 0131 5 56 55 65 | www.scotsmanscreenings.com*

LIVE MUSIC

CABARET VOLTAIRE ⭐ (110 B2) (*M F5*)
There are performances by new British bands on most days in the subterranean heart of the Old Town. After the gigs, the club, with its three small stages, turns into one of the best dance addresses in town. *Performances from 7pm and 11pm | entrance free of up to £14 | 36 Blair Street | www.thecabaretvoltaire.com*

JAZZ BAR (110 B3) (*M F5*)
Three gigs take place every evening in the groovy cellar with its small stage. It becomes funkier after 9pm at weekends when a DJ takes over. A small admission fee is charged for each performance. ● *Teatime Acoustic Tue–Sat 6pm–8.30pm, Early Gig daily 8.30–11.30pm, Late Night live 11.30pm–3am | 1a Chambers Street | www.thejazzbar.co.uk*

INSIDER TIP ▶ ROYAL OAK (110 B3) (*M G5*)
During the day, this is about as empty as a pub can be. But later in the evening, the two small bars on the ground floor and in the basement fill up and the air vibrates with the sound of strings, bows and – usually smoky – voices. Folk music so exciting it will even make your beer froth. *Daily 9am–2am | 1 Infirmary Street*

SANDY BELL'S ⭐ ● (110 A3) (*M F6*)
A simple pub that does not serve food near Greyfriars Cemetery. However, it really comes alive in the afternoon and evening when local and international folk-music stars get together for a jam session. Guitars, singing: Celtic lifestyle at its best. *Daily 11am–1am | 25 Forrest Road*

GAY & LESBIAN

Edinburgh's 'pink triangle' is located between Broughton Street, Leith Walk and East London Street with cafés, pubs and restaurants. The gay and lesbian crowd meets in the 1980s-style gay nightclub *CC Blooms (Thu–Tue 8pm–3am, sometimes to 5am | free admission | 23 Greenside Place).* Mariners *(admission from £5.50 | 40 Commercial Street | Leith | tel. 0131 5 55 56 22)* in a converted church is the best address for a gay chillout lounge; it also has evenings just for men or women on various days at varying times. *www.edinburghgayscene.com*

THEATRE & CLASSICAL MUSIC

FESTIVAL THEATRE ⭐ (110 B3) (*M G6*)
This is the most prestigious theatre in Edinburgh, not only during the Festival. Modern dance, opera, drama – all the top names perform here. Stylish mixture of an old theatre building and modern glass architecture. *Admission £5–55 | 13–29 Nicolson Street | www.eft.co.uk*

A truly regal auditorium: the magnificent King's Theatre

KING'S THEATRE (109 E5) (⌘ D7)

This theatre seems to have sprung out of an old picture book: wood, marble and gold leaf create an elegant setting for plays, musicals, comedies and opera. There are pubs next door so you will be able to knock back a quick pint during the interval. This is where Sean Connery made his first appearance as an actor. *Admission from £11 | 2 Leven Street | www.eft.co.uk*

PLAYHOUSE (106 B4) (⌘ G3)

A great variety of international stars ranging from Steely Dan and Tom Waits to Katie Melua, as well as travelling musical shows, appear in this large auditorium with 3000 seats on Calton Hill. This is also a popular venue for well-known British stand-up comedians. *Admission from £11 | 18–22 Greenside Place | www.edinburgh playhouse.org.uk*

ROYAL LYCEUM THEATRE COMPANY (109 E3) (⌘ D6)

The classics and occasionally contemporary plays are performed in a beautiful Victorian building from 1883. It is even said that a ghost haunts the gallery. As many as eight plays are staged annually making the Royal Lyceum, in its own words, the largest dramatic theatre in Scotland. *Admission from £13 | Grindlay Street | www. lyceum.org.uk*

TRAVERSE THEATRE (109 E3) (⌘ D5)

This is the centre of contemporary Scottish theatre. Fans of these types of performances will find what they are looking for on the stage in the cellar; those who are not so enthusiastic but still want to sample Edinburgh's theatrical air should at least visit the INSIDER TIP *Traverse Bar Café*. Popular Fringe Festival meeting point. *Admission free or up to £20 | www. traverse.co.uk*

USHER HALL (109 E2) (⌘ D5)

This magnificent circular theatre was renovated a few years ago and is the venue for the most important concerts of classical music during the Edinburgh Festival. At other times, there are concerts with symphony orchestras, jazz stars and rock bands. The main organ, which was also recently restored, is a real treasure. *Admission from £16 | corner of Lothian Road and Castle Steps | www.usherhall. co.uk*

WHERE TO STAY

In spite of its relatively small size, Edinburgh has a wide variety of hotels with a total of 23,000 beds, many of them in small guesthouses. But even that number is hardly enough during the Festival weeks in summer and at Hogmanay (31 December). Then everything is hopelessly booked out.

There is a good selection of charming, traditional grand hotels and trendy boutique hotels in the luxury segment. They might be a bit more than your average holiday budget but most of them also have a brasserie, café or nightclub on the premises that make it possible for people not staying there to take a look inside. You will have no trouble reaching your Bed & Breakfast accommodation by bus if it is a little bit out of the centre. In hotels and guesthouses you will probably have to pay around £6 for a continental breakfast or £12 for the Scottish variety.

Two or three-star hotel chains have little individual character and will probably even make you forget what a magnificent city you are in while you are there overnight. That makes staying in one of the Georgian townhouses from the 18th and 19th centuries even more recommendable, where you stay in typically high-ceilinged rooms and can enjoy personal hospitality – along with sometimes draughty sash windows

There is a huge choice of boutique hotels and guesthouses – but Edinburgh is always bursting at the seams during the Festival

and thick quilts on the bed. The widely varying prices of double rooms in these hotels in the former homes of the wealthier classess *(£70–140)*, however, do usually include breakfast. A shield with stars issued by the Scottish Tourism Society at the door of a hotel is a useful aid in determining its quality.

The prices of rooms can easily double during the Edinburgh International and the Fringe Festival, over public holidays and when international rugby games are scheduled – especially in August and December. There is usually a considerable reduction in prices otherwise between October and March. If you look at the websites of the boutique hotels, you will often find amazing special offers! Other good sources include: *www.hotelreview scotland.com, www.stayinedinburgh.net*

You would really expect tartan: stylish rooms in the Rutland Hotel

HOTELS: EXPENSIVE

CHANNINGS ⭐ (104 B–C4) (📖 B3)

Relaxed, elegant and tasteful surroundings with a heroic-historical touch. Some of the five houses from the Edwardian Belle Époque that were combined to create a peacefully located townhouse idyll belonged to the Antarctic explorer Sir Ernest Schackleton. Two suites have documentary evidence of this with photos taken on the famous Endurance expedition to the South Pole. Outstanding restaurant. The hotel belongs to a local group *(www.townhousecompany.com)* that also owns three similar hotels. *41 rooms | 12–16 Learmouth Gardens | tel. 0131 3 15 22 26 | www.channings.co.uk*

CHESTER RESIDENCE ● (108 C2) (📖 B5)

Large apartments in Edwardian terrace houses in the peaceful West End. High ceilings, kitchen, cool design and sound system, luxuriously furnished in muted colours. The reception is staffed around the clock, arranges breakfast and can help out with almost any wish. Guests feel like they are staying in an upper-class home with discrete personnel. *10 apartments | 9 Rothesay Place | tel. 0131 2 26 20 75 | www.chester-residence.com*

HOTEL DU VIN ⭐ (110 A–B3) (📖 F6)

This medium-sized, luxury boutique hotel that opened not so long ago successfully blends the charm of a listed building in the Old Town with the requirements of a modern hotel such as the discreet insertion of double glazing into the original two-part sash windows. The rooms are luxurious but practical, the delightful details elegant, the service exceptional. There is an exquisitely-stocked wine bar and a room for whisky tasting. The bistro restaurant has the intimate atmosphere of a wine store; the inner courtyard on the other hand provides a modern, almost minimalistic contrast to the surrounding Old Town. *47 rooms | 11 Bristo Place | tel. 0131 2 47 49 00 | www.hotelduvin.com*

MALMAISON (109 F1) (*M1 L1*)

This building, which looks like a city *palais*, at the port in Leith is one of the older boutique hotels. It was built in 1833 as a home for sailors and is now the flagship hotel of the Scottish Malmaison company – a somewhat old-fashioned *grandseigneur* of the hotel business. Here and there, the luxury is a bit frayed, but the grand-hotel atmosphere has been preserved in spite of the house's boutique character. The guests live directly on the water not far from the three restaurants that have been awarded Michelin stars and are typical of the new lifestyle in the old port. *100 rooms | 1 Tower Place | Leith | tel. 01314 69 50 00 | www.malmaison-edinburgh.com*

LE MONDE (109 F1) (*M1 E4*)

This luxurious boutique hotel on Scotland's most exclusive shopping street has received several awards since opening. And, it deserves them! The furnishings of the suites are styled on dream cities around the world. However, the rest is a bit bombastic for the sober Georgian style of the street: the flamboyant *Paris* restaurant is Belle Époque, *Shanghai* – the nightclub with a DJ – stays open until 3am and attracts the student crowd *(admission £5)*; breakfast is served in *Milan* and the 'in' crowd congregate in the *Brasserie Vienna*. *Très chic*! *18 rooms | 16 George Street | tel. 01312 70 39 00 | www.lemondehotel.co.uk*

RUTLAND ★ (109 D2) (*M1 D5*)

The Scottish 'Style Awards' named this small luxury boutique hotel best in its class immediately after it was opened. The location in the West End opens up views of the neighbouring castle and Calton Hill on the horizon. The rooms are individually designed, not over-decorated. By the way, this is where the father of antiseptic surgery, Joseph Lister, once lived. The brasserie restaurant is pleasant, the nightclub

The One Below (daily until 3am) INSIDER TIP ▶ with one of the still rare iBars – more or less a touch-screen surface for painting and writing with your fingers – is one of the most popular top lounges at the moment and the guests are usually actually older than 25. *12 rooms | 1–3 Rutland Street | tel. 01312 29 34 02 | www.the rutlandhotel.com*

HOTELS: MODERATE

BANK HOTEL ★ (110 B2) (*M1 F5*)

Each of the themed rooms in this renovated Neoclassicist corner building that was originally opened as a bank in 1923 is devoted to a local celebrity such as Robert Burns. This junction on the Royal

MARCO POLO HIGHLIGHTS

Mile is very lively as is the bar on the ground floor where breakfast, which is included in the room price, is also served. Princes Street is just two minutes away. The perfect place for a romantic city trip! *9 rooms | 1 South Bridge | tel. 0131 5 56 99 40 | www.festival-inn.co.uk*

CANDLEMAKER ROW (110 A3) (*F6*)

This flat in an 18th-century house near Greyfriars Cemetery is intended for a maximum of four people. You can leave the hustle and bustle of the Old Town outside the thick walls of this modern, comfortable and well-equipped flat. It is best to reserve for a week or for days that are free between two other bookings. *Weekly rate £300–690 | 48/1 Candlemaker Row | tel. 0131 5 38 03 52 | www.edinburgh selfcatering.webeden.co.uk*

EQ2-FOUNTAINCOURT APARTMENTS

You can live very comfortably in these apartments at four different locations in the West End of the inner city: kitchen, luxurious bathroom, home-entertainment system and even a parking space in the heart of town. The price is reduced according to the length of your stay. Breakfast packs for four can be purchased as an extra. *150 flats | tel. 0131 6 22 66 77 | www.fountaincourtapartments.com*

HOLIDAY INN EXPRESS CITY CENTER (106 B4) (*F3*)

The chain's most central hotel is located in Broughton below Calton Hill. Six storeys with spotless rooms but not a great deal of atmosphere. *161 rooms | Picardy Place | tel. 0131 5 58 23 00 | www.hieedinburgh.co.uk*

HUDSON HOTEL (109 D2) (*D5*)

The former post office between Charlotte Square and the west end of Princes Street has been invested with the cool charm of a city hotel. The style harmonises with the location, the service is reserved; business people and visitors seem to appreciate that. Breakfast is taken in the bar. This is a INSIDERTIP top location where the Old Town, New Town and Dean Village meet. The bus to the airport leaves almost from the doorstep. *30 rooms | 9–11 Hope Street | tel. 0131 2 47 70 00 | www.thehudsonhotel. co.uk*

STEVENSON HOUSE (105 E5) *(⬦ D4)*
You will have an exclusive home-away-from-home in this house where Robert Louis Stevenson lived from the age of six. The only double room *(£100 year round)* has an antique four-poster bed while the breakfast is more in keeping with our times and includes sourdough bread and muesli – the lady of the house is German. The Georgian house with the friendly personal touch also has two single rooms and is located in the centre of the New Town. *3 rooms | 17 Heriot Row | tel. 0131 5 56 18 96 | www.stevenson-house.co.uk*

LUXURY HOTELS

Balmoral (110 B1) *(⬦ F4)*
The twenty suites – including three royal suites – are the best that Edinburgh has to offer apart from those in certain boutique hotels. The castle-like building forms a focal point on Princes Street; the large clock on the tower is always two minutes fast (except on New Year's Eve) so that passengers will not miss their train from the neighbouring Waverley Station. The rooms are decorated in a restrained elegance; the rest is marble and crystal. The doorman is Scottish, *Hadrian's Brasserie*, continental, the *Number One* restaurant has a Michelin star and also serves a fine selection of vegetarian dishes. *188 rooms | £320 (double room)– £2000 (suite) | 1 Princes Street | tel. 0131 5 56 24 14 | www.the balmoralhotel.com*

Caledonian Hilton ☽ (109 D2) *(⬦ D 5)*
The second grand hotel on Princes Street is located at the other, the western, end of the long thoroughfare although it is only three house numbers away. Not quite as dazzling as the Balmoral, but just a little bit more authentically Scottish. Decorated with the colours of the highland heaths, the hotel also has a Sean Connery Suite – the actor likes to stay here when he is in town. Two restaurants and fabulous views of the castle and Firth of Forth. *251 rooms | double room from £150 | Princes Street | tel. 0131 2 22 88 88 | www.hilton.co.uk/caledonian*

The Scotsman ★ (110 B1) *(⬦ F5)*
Five-star, luxurious boutique hotel with a somewhat labyrinthine layout. It is hard to believe that the leading newspaper *The Scotsman* was produced here for a century. The colourful leaded windows and marble that welcome you as you enter will give you a feeling of the Edwardian Belle Époque. Located on the doorstep of the Old Town on North Bridge, it looks like a fairytale castle on a drawbridge. Cool stainless-steel pool, cosy miniature cinema, superb restaurant and what is possibly the most opulent brasserie in Edinburgh, the ● *North Bridge (separate entrance) | www.northbridge brasserie.com. 69 rooms | £260 (double room)–£1800 (suite) | 20 North Bridge | tel. 0131 5 56 55 65 | www.thescotsman hotel.co.uk*

Refined – and inexpensive – elegance does exist in Edinburgh, too: Ailsa Craig Hotel

TAILOR'S HALL (110 A3) (*ø F5*)
Some visitors feel right at home in the nocturnal bustle of Edinburgh's Old Town. This three-star hotel is the perfect choice for tourists who want to live in a 400-year-old building with contrastingly modern, sober rooms and mingle with all the locals at the rustic, lively hotel bar. *42 rooms | 139 Cowgate | tel. 0131 6 22 68 01 | www.festival-inns.co.uk*

HOTELS: BUDGET

53 FREDERICK STREET (105 E5) (*ø E4*)
This guesthouse (breakfast is included) in a Georgian house in the centre of the New Town offers traditional elegance and large rooms. Peaceful surroundings, attentive and friendly hosts. *4 rooms | 53 Frederick Street | tel. 0131 2 26 27 52 | www.53frederickstreet.com*

AILSA CRAIG HOTEL (107 D4) (*ø H3*)
This typical townhouse hotel in the New Town was built by none other than William Playfair, one of the greatest Scottish architects of his day, in 1820. It is located in a pleasant, leafy residential area on the northern side of Calton Hill; perfect for sunset strolls with a view of the city. Large, clean, simple rooms. Good value for money. Bus 15 leaves from London Road just around the corner for INSIDER TIP mysterious Rosslyn Chapel south of the city where Dan Brown set the end of his best-seller *The Da Vinci Code*. *17 rooms | 24 Royal Terrace | tel. 0131 5 56 50 55 | www.townhousehotels.co.uk/hotels/ailsacraig.html*

BALMORE HOUSE
(109 E5) (*ø D7*)
Cheerful, immaculate, inexpensive guesthouse with several large rooms a good ten minutes from West End. Victorian Balmore House is decorated in the British style with thick carpets and papered walls while the affiliated neighbouring *Bowmore House* has a Scandinavian touch with wooden floors and light-coloured furniture. A substantial breakfast is included in the

price. *7 rooms | 34 Gilmore Place | tel. 0131 2 21 13 31 | www.balmore-holidays.co.uk*

CLAREMONT (106 A2) (⌖ F2)

Two Georgian houses on one of the typical semicircular streets were joined to create a hotel with high, light-filled rooms that are not over-furnished. Lovely area in the northern part of the New Town. *22 rooms | 14–15 Claremont Street | tel. 0131 5 56 14 87 | www.claremont-hotel.co.uk*

FREDERICK HOUSE
(105 E5) (⌖ E4)

Former offices were converted to create the rooms – most of them spacious – of this five-storey Georgian New Town hotel. Typical of many townhouses, it is a bit run-down and not really adequately equipped. Top residential location and tasty à-la-carte breakfast in the restaurant on the other side of the street. *45 rooms | 42 Frederick Street | tel. 0131 2 26 19 99 | www.town househotels.co/uk/hotels/frederick.html*

GRASSMARKET HOTEL ★
(110 A3) (⌖ E5)

This hotel is located at the hottest spot in town so you should ask for a room at the back if you want to spend a quiet night. The hotel is at least worth its two stars: the rooms have en suite bathrooms, are simple and clean. The location where hangings used to take place and not far away from an Irish pub *(Biddy Mulligan)* is unbeatable. *45 rooms | 94–96 Grass-market | tel. 0131 2 20 22 29 | www.festival-inns.co.uk*

IBIS CENTRE
(110 B2) (⌖ F5)

It would be hard to find a hotel in this price category in a more central location in the Old Town. The hotel offers spotless accommodation including six double rooms suitable for disabled guests. *99 rooms | 6 Hunter Square | tel. 0131 2 40 70 00 | www.ibishotel.com*

STRAVEN GUEST HOUSE
(113 D1) (⌖ 0)

This small, homely guesthouse is located in Portobello, Edinburgh's sandy beach. You will enjoy a tasty breakfast and pleasant, not too plush, rooms and fresh sea air. The bus takes a good 20 minutes to reach Princes Street. *4 rooms | 3 Brunstone Road North | tel. 0131 69 55 80 | www.straven guesthouse.com | buses 15, 26*

LOW BUDGET

▶ There are a large number of hostel beds in Edinburgh. The *Belford Hostel* in Dean Village is a former church with a house bar *(98 dormitory beds, 7 small rooms | £18/person | 6–8 Douglas Gardens | tel. 0131 25 62 09)*. The five-star *Smartcity Hostel (630 rooms, all with bath | £12/person | 50 Blackfriars Street | (*) tel. 0870 892 30 00)* is enormous, completely modern, and in the heart of the Old Town. It also has a somewhere to put bicycles and luggage storage facilities.

▶ The *Eurolodge* in the West End offers magnificent Georgian architecture and an interior to match – as well as a past history as a hospital: that's why some of the rooms have as many as 20 beds. *(100 beds, including 4 double rooms | £15/person | 25 Palmerston Place | tel. 0131 2 20 51 41)*.

▶ You will often find very attractive last-minute offers ('hot dates') for the expensive hotels on the Internet *(www.hotelreviewsscotland.com)*.

WALKING TOURS

The tours are marked in green in the street atlas, pull-out map and on the back cover

1 WATER OF LEITH WALKWAY

There are many hidden secrets in Edinburgh – the Water of Leith is one of the more conspicuous ones. Not many visitors to the city think about following its meandering course through various villages. But it's well worth exploring! Go down into the small wooded gorge, wander through Dean Village, and you'll soon leave the hustle and bustle of the Royal Mile and the castle behind you. The entire route is around 12 miles long, but there are many places along the way where you can interrupt it.

If you are staying in the New Town, walk towards Circus Place until you reach Kerr Street or take bus 24 or 29. The Leith lies hidden only a stone's throw away beneath Kerr Street Bridge. But before you make your way down the steps to the water, you should make a short detour to Stockbridge. Kerr Street soon leads into Raeburn Place → p. 62 with its many small shops. An old barber's, a fishmonger's and second-hand shops invite you to go window-shopping and rummage around. After that, you can go back to the river and make your way down to its banks. Once there, you will find yourself engulfed in green. Wrought-iron fences frame the

Photo: Stockbridge

A walk along the Water of Leith through Edinburgh's villages, on a poetic paperchase in the Old Town or over the hills to a pub

banks frequented by blue kingfishers and grey herons. You can catch a fleeting glimpse of the old houses on **Dean Terrace** through the treetops. Looking south, follow the signposts to the galleries on the east bank and, a few minutes later, you will be standing in front of **St Bernhard's Well**. The lovely temple with the figure of Hygeia, the Greek goddess of cleanliness, was donated by a well-off

benefactor and marks the place where and ancient spring once stood. A little further on, the slender supports of **Dean Bridge** soar into the sky. Many firms in the creative sector have opened offices in the former mills below. The scene is reminiscent of a watercolour by William Turner. The bridge was designed by the Scottish architect Thomas Telford (1832) and is an eloquent illustration of Edinburgh's abrupt changes in level. There were mills and bread ovens here in Dean Village → p. 47 almost 1000 years ago. The depictions of the paddles used to remove bread from the ovens on some house walls are a sign of the bakers' guild. The path now moves away from the river for a while, past millstones and down Millers Row, along rural lanes with half-timbered houses and then back to the stream again. Relax and enjoy the meandering course and then climb up out of the gorge to the two galleries opposite each other on Belford Road. Dean Gallery → p. 47 and the Scottish National Gallery of Modern Art → p. 48 are Classicist temple constructions and, seeing that admission is free, you should make a break in your hike for a short visit and enjoy a cup of tea and a piece of cake. On no account should you miss Dean Cemetery → p. 47 behind Dean Gallery where you can find the tomb of William Playfair (1759–1823), the architect whose Classicist buildings are responsible for Edinburgh's reputation as the 'Athens of the North'.

When you leave the cemetery, turn right along Dean Path. Queensferry Road and Belford Road merge to form Queensferry Street that leads into the west end of Princes Street. Half way along Queensferry Street you will be confronted with an outstanding example of Edinburgh's different architectural styles: Melville Street on the right is characterised by a harmonious row of Georgian townhouse façades with a stylised Gothic church looming up in contrast behind them. The round Romanesque church on Randolph Place – today the National Archives – lies on the left. A little more than 600 ft away, the Caledonian Hilton → p. 79 dominates the cityscape in the West End. And you will once again be able to gaze up at Edinburgh Castle → p. 30. Information under www.waterofleith.org.uk

2 LITERATURE TOUR ALONG WELL-TRODDEN PATHS

It is impossible to overlook the places where poetry and prose were written in a city that Unesco named the first World City of Literature in 2004. Quite the contrary, you will encounter such places wherever you go; you just have to walk through the labyrinth of old lanes – called *closes* and *wynds* – that branch off the Royal Mile. Take a couple of hours to track down around 300 years of literature.

The walk begins up at the Royal Mile → p. 35 where Ramsay Land branches off Castlehill. The white octagonal towers with Scottish baronial elements from the 18th century, trimmed with red bands of sandstone, are known as Ramsay Garden. The poet Allan Ramsay (1686–1758) lived in the Old Town high above Princes Street Gardens → p. 44, with a view over the New Town and as far as the Firth of Forth, that are still so popular today. Ramsay was one of the first men of letters of the Scottish age of Enlightenment following the union with England in 1707. In 1725, he founded the 'Easy Club' literary circle. The members met in pubs and you may also want to interrupt your stroll for a pint or two.

Back to the Royal Mile, which is called Lawnmarket here, you pass a typical six-storey residential building from the 17th century: Gladstone's Land. It belongs to the National Trust and gives an insight into how the wealthy merchant Gladstone resided and who were the tenants in his house. Riddle's Court is just a few steps further down the Mile. This is where David Hume (1711–76) lived – the philosopher, political-economist, atheist and civil-rights theoretician, a friend of the market-economy philosopher Adam Smith and an important guiding intellectual force for

Immanuel Kant. Hume's Monument is just around the corner on the Royal Mile. **James Court** lies opposite at the end of a lane. The inner courtyard is surrounded by renovated, five-storey residential buildings and there is a pub called the *Jolly Judge (7 James Court)* in the cellar. The journalist and author James Boswell (1740–95) rented a flat here. He had left his wife and child behind when he went to look for a publisher for his works in the city. To his dismay, he was forced to work in the legal profession and 'rewarded' himself for this with a free and easy nightlife. He met Voltaire and Rousseau and one of the highlights of his literary ambitions was his encounter with England's most celebrated intellectual, Samuel Johnson, in Edinburgh in 1763. The famous lexicographer – a dictionary specialist – writer and critic subsequently set out on an arduous trip to the Hebrides with Boswell in August 1773 which was to last for several months. INSIDER TIP The books written by the two men still make great reading today and Boswell's biography of Johnson, who he idolised, is considered one of the most famous in English literature. Sit down in the Jolly Judge and browse through Boswell's book.

This is followed by **Lady Stair's Close** where the Scottish national poet Robert Burns (1759–96) spent a winter. Burns had just written his first volume in Scots under the influence of the young, extremely talented, Robert Ferguson (1750–74) whose striding bronze figure has been placed in the lower section of the Royal Mile. Burns introduced Old Town characters such as market women and pub owners into poetry. Buy a volume of Burns' verses in Scots in one of the bookshops; you will be surprised at how easy they are to understand. There is a small **museum** → p. 39 devoted to Edinburgh's most important writers in Lady Stair's Close.

Sought-after accommodation: the octagonal towers in Ramsay Garden

The plaque proves it: J. K. Rowling wrote Harry Potter in the Buffet King Restaurant

Deacon William Brodie moved into **Brodie's Close** on the other side of the Mile in 1780. During the day, he was a city councillor and ran a carpenter's workshop but he was also so excessively involved in Edinburgh's nightlife that he was always hard up. He was forced to relieve his clients of their valuables. He got caught and thousands of spectators watched him being hung from the gallows he had created so efficiently as a carpenter a few years before. He died on the Mile diagonally across from the pub that now bears his name. The place where Brodie was left hanging was the site of the Tollbooth Prison that is now only marked by the so-called **Heart of Midlothian** → p. 33 in the pavement. This brings us to Walter Scott. Scotland's famous novelist immortalised the medieval prison in his book of the same name and even acquired a cell door as a souvenir when it was demolished in 1817. A few feet away, you should enter **St Giles Cathedral** → p. 38

on High Street to see how Edinburgh honours its writers of life on the city's streets: Burns has been given a memorial window and Robert Louis Stevenson (1850–94), who turned William Brodie's double life – something not completely untypical of Edinburgh – into his novel *Dr. Jekyll and Mr Hyde*, is remembered with a sculpted plaque.

You should not miss two other lanes on the other side of the street. The name of **Advocate's Close**, from where you have the lovely view towards the New Town, reminds us that Stevenson, Scott and Boswell were lawyers. ● **Real Mary King's Close** on the other hand was built over and is under the ground today and gives an impression of how things were in the year of the plague 1645 when the street and the people living on it were walled in along with Gladstone's Land. A tour of the closes offers some shocking revelations about the life of the 50,000 inhabitants of the Old Town, crowded together, fighting against hunger, filth and disease. *(Tours daily every 20 minutes, April–Oct 10am–9pm, Aug 9am–9pm, Nov–March 10am–5pm | £10.50 | www.realmarykings close.com).*

Now head towards Cowgate, the road that runs parallel to the Mile to the south. Walter Scott was born on Guthrie Street while this was still named College Wynd. Looking over South Bridge you can see the lanes of Infirmary Street where Scott attended the Royal High School; today, this is a university building. This was the site of the Old Royal Infirmary where the writer William Ernest Henley lay for two years after one of his legs had been amputated. He became the model for the pirate with the wooden leg, Long John Silver, in Stevenson's novel *Treasure Island*. INSIDER TIP *The Buffet King Restaurant (formerly Nicholson's | Budget)* where J.K. Rowling worked on one of her Harry Potter novels is just around the corner at 6a Nicholson Street. Whenever her daughter was asleep in her pram, she went there to write: "They were friendly enough to let me stay there with a single espresso. You have no idea how much you can write in two hours." Edinburgh really loves its writers. Further information: *www.edinburghliterarypubtour.co.uk* or *www.edinburghbookloverstour.com*

3 OVER THE VOLCANO TO SCOTLAND'S OLDEST PUB

Similar to Rome and Lisbon, Edinburgh has seven volcanic hills. The difference is that only here does the terrain tempt one to go on a tour which has the feeling of the Highlands – in the centre of town! After the steep ascent to Arthur's Seat, you will be rewarded for your efforts by a view of an idyllic lake and a beer in Edinburgh's oldest watering hole.

Setting out to the south-east of the Parliament buildings, you arrive at Queen's Drive which winds around the entire massif, after around 700 ft. You will find the start to the climb around 300 ft further on near the 'Danger! Rocks' sign.

Stage one takes you up steeply over a good path towards the south below and along Salisbury Crags, a procession of 150 ft high basalt columns that can be seen from far away. Walking anticlockwise, you will gradually lose sight of the wonderful view of the Parliament. After a bit more than half a mile and shortly reaching Queen's Drive once again, turn sharply to the north (left, climb over a small swell and follow one of the paths through a long valley. Now, at the latest, you will feel that you have left the city behind you and are really out in the Highlands.

When you reach the end of the valley, stay to the right of some small cliffs and look for the 🌿 remains of a little chapel; take a break and admire the view of the city and sea. After this, a good path leads you in the other direction to the south. You hike along the contour of the hill and then upwards until you reach the main ascent route to the peak, Arthur's Seat → p. 29 that leads up for a short distance to the right. When you reach the top, you are 823 ft above sea level so that you can make out Queen's Drive in the distance and 571 ft below. You will be able to enjoy a 🌿 view over the entire city of Edinburgh, the other hills surrounding the city and the Firth of Forth. The descent on the east side is short and ends at Queen's Drive. Only around 600 ft away, you will see the glittering water of Duddingston Loch. To the north of the lake, on the Causeway, the Sheep Heid Inn → p. 70, the oldest pub in Scotland that opened its doors in 1360, will beckon you in to have a drink: *Mary Queen of Scots was here!*

TRAVEL WITH KIDS

Children can have a thrilling time in Edinburgh. The tours through the *Dungeons* chamber of horrors at Waverley Station however are only suitable for hardened teenagers accompanied by adults – not for young children. The evening *Ghost Tours* through the lanes of the city are less scary.

DEEP SEA WORLD ● (112 C1) (*∅ 0*)

A conveyor belt takes visitors through a kind of aquarium with sharks, rays, schools of colourful fish and seals. The most fascinating aspect of the almost 10-mile excursion to North Queensferry – at least for parents – will probably be the train journey across the Firth of Forth Bridge, the most famous cantilever bridge in the world. You can include a 45-minute boat trip from South Queensferry directly under the bridge *(March–Oct)* and spend one-and-a-half hours on Inchcolm Island. There are wonderful abbey ruins on the island and many sea birds and inquisitive seals on the shore from April/May. *Mon–Fri 10am–5pm, Sat, Sun 10am–6pm | entrance fee £11.75, children over the age of 3 £8 | North Queensferry | www.deepseaworld.com | Fife Circle Line from Waverley or Haymarket*

EDINBURGH ZOO (112 C2) (*∅ 0*)

The landscape of the hilly zoo is really beautiful. You should start your visit by taking the shuttle to the top of the zoo and then wander down the hill past the koalas, rhinoceroses and other animals. Children love the INSIDER TIP penguin parade *(April–Aug 2.15pm)*. Don't set off without a packed lunch! *April–Sept daily 9am–6pm, Oct and March daily 9am–5pm, Nov–Feb daily 9am–4.30pm | admission £14, children over the age of 3 £9.50 | Corstorphine Road | Murrayfield | www.edinburghzoo.org.uk | buses 12, 26, 31*

HORROR TOURS

Sooner or later, somebody will thrust a colourful flyer into your hand and entice you into the dark corners of town. Quite a few amateur actors make their living from scaring the wits out of visitors for a couple of hours. A bit like a historical ghost train, professionally performed with costumes and makeup – not for the fainthearted but exciting for bright kids. *Mercat Walking Tours from £9 | tel. 0131 557 64 64 | www.mercattours.com; City of the Dead Tours: from £9 | tel. 0131 225*

A day with the penguins at the zoo, take the train to the Aquarium or Science Museum – and meet some ghosts in the evening

90 44 | www.blackhart.uk.com; Witchery Tours: from £9 | tel. 0131 225 67 45 | www.witcherytours.com

MUSEUM OF CHILDHOOD
(110 B2) (*Ø G5*)

This is actually more of a museum for adults who have remained young because the tin soldiers, Barbies and a hotchpotch of exhibits are arranged chronologically and not presented interactively. However, the whole family will profit from a visit if the parents tell stories about the exhibits that have been collected with such loving care. *Mon–Sat 10am–5pm, Sun noon–5pm | 42 High Street, Royal Mile | www.museum ofchildhood.org.uk*

OUR DYNAMIC EARTH ★
(111 D2) (*Ø H5*)

The science museum in a gigantic tent construction is a real hit with schoolchildren.

The journey through time begins with the Big Bang, 14 billion years ago. Earthquake simulator, volcano eruption scenario, a virtual trip through the world of glaciers and the centre of the earth. Global climatic scenarios can be investigated in the 'Future' section.

The affiliated *Earthscape Scotland Gallery* explains the geology of the country; there is a fine example outside – the gallery is next to the volcanic peak, Arthur's Seat. The geology lesson is also intended to be a homage to the Edinburgh resident James Hutton (1726–97) who is considered the founder of that particular science. It is high time for the scenario under the tent to be renovated but this is still at the planning stage. *Nov–March Wed–Sun 10am–5pm, April–June, Sept, Oct daily 10am–5pm, July, Aug 10am–6pm | admission £12.90, children over the age of 3 £8.95 | 4 Holyrood Road | www.dynamicearth.co.uk*

FESTIVALS & EVENTS

It is not without reason that Edinburgh bears the epithet 'Festival City'. Things really come to life in August when several festivals are held at the same time and attract thousands of visitors. Further information under *www.eventsedinburgh. co.uk* and *www.edinburghfestivals.co.uk*.

PUBLIC HOLIDAYS

1 Jan *(New Year's Day)*, **2 Jan**, **Good Friday**, **last Mon in May** *(Spring Bank Holiday)*, **1st Mon in August** *(Summer Bank Holiday)*, **30 Nov** *(St Andrew's Day)*, **25 Dec**, **26 Dec**. If Christmas or New Year's Day fall on Sat or Sun, Mon is a public holiday.

EVENTS

JANUARY
25 Jan: Robert Burns' birthday is celebrated in restaurants with haggis and whisky, and his verses recited on ▶ *Burns Night*.

MARCH/APRIL
Last week in March–mid-April: The ▶ INSIDER TIP *Ceilidh Culture Festival* is a Celtic celebration of music and literature.

APRIL
The 2-week ▶ *International Science Festival,* with its more than 200 individual events, focuses on technology and science. *www. sciencefestival.co.uk*

30 April: The ▶ INSIDER TIP *Beltane Fire Festival* is a Celtic mega-party on Calton Hill. More than 12,000 people welcome the summer every year with bonfires and drums in ecstatic mood – a great way to dance into May.

MAY
Last week in May: ▶ *The Imaginate Festival* is Great Britain's largest theatre festival for children and youths.

JUNE
Mid-June: The 4-day ▶ *Royal Highland Show*, held near the airport, is Scotland's largest agricultural show. *www.royalhigh landshow.org*

Mid-June: Stars like Sean Connery, Tilda Swinton and Robert Carlyle are often patrons at the twelve-day ▶ *Edinburgh International Film Festival. www.edfilmfest. org.uk*

Edinburgh is a stage for cultural events throughout the year: mystic festivals, theatre, science and even one for the *haggis*

JULY

End of July: The ▶ *Edinburgh Jazz & Blues Festival* lasts 10 days. *www.edinburgh jazzfestival.co.uk*

AUGUST/SEPTEMBER

The ▶ ★ *Edinburgh International Festival (3 weeks from mid-Aug, www.eif.co.uk)* with its classic programme and the ▶ ★ ● *Edinburgh Festival Fringe (3 weeks in August, www.edfringe.com)* with countless theatre and comedy productions are considered the world's largest cultural events. The ▶ *Edinburgh Military Tattoo (3 weeks in Aug, www.edinburgh-tattoo.co.uk)* with the castle as its backdrop is the most spectacular military-band festival worldwide. The ▶ *Edinburgh Art Festival (4 weeks in Aug and Sept, www.edinburghartfestival. com)* in the city's museums and galleries is a relatively new event. The ▶ *Edinburgh International Book* festival in the 2nd half of Aug has more than 800 events. *www. edbookfest.co.uk*
The ethnic carnival in Leith, the ▶ *Edinburgh Mela*, heats up the last week in Aug. *www. edinburgh-mela.co.uk*

OCTOBER

Last week in Oct: Scots love telling stories and celebrate this aspect of their culture at the ▶ *Scottish International Storytelling Festival* held in the Story Telling Centre.

DECEMBER

▶ *Edinburgh's Christmas* is Great Britain's largest Christmas market with an ice skating rink; held in Princes Street Gardens. 29 Dec–1 Jan: The popular 4-day New Year's celebration is known as ▶ *Hogmanay*. The highlight is the New Year's Eve street party (admission fee!) where tens of thousands celebrate throughout the city. *www.edin burghhogmanay.org*

LINKS, BLOGS, APPS & MORE

LINKS

▶ en.wikipedia.org/wiki/Portal: Scotland History, politics, geography and things to do – here you can find the answers to many a question about Scotland!

▶ www.edinburghspotlight.com This website publishes tips, *reviews* and blogs about culture, food, children, access for the disabled, sport and daily excursions.

All you need to know about the capital city, and up-to-date – take a look at it!

▶ www.stniniansday.co.uk/scotlands_story.php The history of the country is told through short portraits of 60 important Scots, from a restrained religious point of view

▶ www.edinburghfestivals.co.uk The official Edinburgh festivals website for tickets, news and reviews to help you plan a trip to the capital and make the most of your stay

BLOGS

▶ www.edinburghwhiskyblog.com New kids on the whisky blog: Two locals in their mid-twenties create a stir in the world of the whisky connoisseur through their blog. If malt ever needed a breath of fresh air, it would get it here. A new, charming facet of the tasty brew.

▶ www.guardian.co.uk/edinburgh Up-to-the-minute journalistic blog on matters affecting the capital city from England's best daily newspaper. At it's very best!

▶ www.theedinburghblog.co.uk This weblog deals with eating and drinking in Edinburgh in great detail. The Twitter entries and the like are particularly up to date.

▶ citycyclingedinburgh.info/bb press Forum for cyclists in the city

Regardless of whether you are still preparing your trip or already in Edinburgh: these addresses will provide you with more information, videos and networks to make your holiday even more enjoyable

BLOGS

▶ www.hiddenorchestra.com/video The Edinburgh Hidden Orchestra Band, with its mix of electronic music and jazz, live during the Edinburgh Festival

▶ www.youtube.com/watch?v= WymV2Bah1Rk Great amateur video portrait of his home town made by a native of Edinburgh

▶ conventionedinburgh.com/video-gallery.html Four professional videos on the official site of the Edinburgh Convention Bureau

APPS

▶ Ian Rankin's Edinburgh You can follow crime writer Ian Rankin through his hometown with this free app. Explanatory and enlightening

▶ Urbanspoon What is being served these days in Edinburgh's restaurants and how does it taste? This app for iPhone, iPad and iPod lets you know

▶ EdinBus The Edinburgh bus timetable with many extra functions as a free app

NETWORK

▶ www.facebook.com/scotlandsforme A large number of tourism businesses have joined forces and this is their very active Facebook link

▶ www.couchsurfing.org/group.html?gid=1251 If you feel like staying with the locals, you should look up the Edinburgh Couchsurfing Group on the Internet

▶ www.thisismyedinburgh.com Twitter, Facebook, blog, forum: this website has information on what's new in the capital and many personal tips

▶ edinburgh.citysocialising.com Even if you don't intend to move to Edinburgh – this is where you can come into contact with many people with a great variety of interests

TRAVEL TIPS

ARRIVAL

✈ Edinburgh Airport *(www.edinburgh airport.com)* is located around 8 mi west of the city centre. The bus trip to Princes Street and Waverley Station takes about half an hour. *Airlink 100* leaves from bus stand 19 every 10 to 20 minutes: the fare is £4. The night bus N22 travels to the city and Leith between 0.47am and 4.13am for £3. Mini-buses start from the car park and will bring you to your doorstep in town for £12.

The most inexpensive means of travel is by the regular 35 line *(www.lothianbuses. com)* from stand 21 for £1.30. It is worth buying a day ticket for £3 if you plan to use the bus service again on the same day. If several people travel together, a taxi from around £18 is another alternative.

🚆 There is at least one direct train to Edinburgh every hour from Kings Cross Station in London *(www.mytrain ticket.co.uk)*. The journey usually takes around 4½ hours; ticket prices vary from £20 to £200.

🚢 From Ireland, several companies run regular services (even up to 8 times a day) between the Emerald Isle and Scotland. The routes between Belfast and Stranraer (a 2hr crossing), Belfast and Cairnryan (2hrs 15mins) and Larne to Troon (2hrs) are probably the most interesting. Alternatively there are ferries to North Wales and Liverpool from Dun Laoghaire and Cork, for example. Compare prices and times: Irish Ferries *(www.irish ferries.com)*, Stena Lines *(www.stenaline. com)*, Brittany Ferries *(www.brittanyferries. com)*.

BANKS & CREDIT CARDS

It is easy to withdraw money from cash dispensers all over the city using your EC card. Shops, hotels, restaurants and most pubs accept standard credit cards. Banks are open from *9am to 5pm Mon–Fri*, except, of course, on public holidays.

CITY TOURS

Lothian Tours, the public service bus, offers five sightseeing trips in open double-decker buses that start from Waverley Station. In addition to the standard 'City Sightseeing' trip with information provided in several languages by way of headphones, the 'Edinburgh Tour' deals with the intellectual universe of the first Unesco City of Literature. The 'MacTours City Tour' is held in a vintage bus and the narrator is onboard *(April–Oct)*. The 'Majestic Tour' is also multilingual and

RESPONSIBLE TRAVEL

It doesn't take a lot to be environmentally friendly whilst travelling. Don't just think about your carbon footprint whilst flying to and from your holiday destination but also about how you can protect nature and culture abroad. As a tourist it is especially important to respect nature, look out for local products, cycle instead of driving, save water and much more. If you would like to find out more about eco-tourism please visit: *www.ecotourism.org*

From arrival to weather

takes guests as far as the coast at Leith. The 'Bus & Boat Tour' goes beyond the city and includes a trip on the Firth of Forth. Ticket prices start at £12 (children £5) and you can hop on and off for 24 hours. *www.edinburghtour.com*

Mercat Tours has a programme of city strolls lasting for several hours at prices starting at £15. There are ten different thematic tours on which the guides deal eloquently with the history and horror stories of the city. *www.mercattours.com*

Allen Fosters Book Lovers Tour is especially recommended for admirers of literature *(www.edinburghbookloverstour.com)* and an evening pub crawl with two entertainers *(www.edinburghliterarypubtour.com)* is another highlight. The ghost tour market is highly competitive and this often leads to calculated kitsch. The most acceptable of the kind is the *Murder and Mystery Tour* with Adam Lyle who was hung in 1871 (£9 | *75 min* | *www.witcherytours.com*).

CURRENCY

In Edinburgh, the currency is the British pound (GBP) divided into 100 pence. Paper money looks different in Scotland than in the rest of Great Britain but has the same value. You can change your Scottish banknotes for English pounds (or euros) at the airport. You will have problems paying with Scottish currency in England; however, it does work the other way round.

CUSTOMS

The allowance when entering Great Britain from countries outside the European Union, including North America, is: 1 litre

BUDGETING

Beer	from £3 *a pint*
Bus	£1.30 *for a single journey*
Fish and chips	from £4.30 *for a take-away serving*
Coffee	from £2 *a cup*
Whisky	from £20 *a bottle*
Cinema	from £8 *a ticket*

of spirits, 200 cigarettes or 100 cigarillos or 50 cigars or 250 g of tobacco, 50 g of perfume or 250 g of eau de toilette and other articles (except gold) to a value of £390. Note that the import of self-defence sprays is prohibited and the import of other weapons requires licences. For more information: *www.hmrc.gov.uk/customs*

DRIVING IN BRITAIN

For travellers from outside the UK: don't forget that you drive on the left in Britain – something that is easy to forget when out in the countryside with no road markings! At roundabouts (which are everywhere in Britain) cars coming from the right have the right of way. British law requires that speed cameras (usually bright yellow) must be easy to spot. The speed limit in built-up areas is 30 mph (50 km/h), 60 mph (96 km/h) on unrestricted single carriage roads and

CURRENCY CONVERTER

$	£	£	$
1	0.70	1	1.40
3	2.10	3	4.20
5	3.50	5	7
13	9.10	13	18.20
40	28	40	56
75	52.50	75	105
120	84	120	168
250	175	250	350
500	350	500	700

For current exchange rates see www.xe.com

70 mph (112 km/h) on motorways and dual carriageways. This is most likely going to be raised to 80 mph (128 km/h) within the foreseeable future.

EDINBURGH & SCOTLAND INFORMATION CENTRE

3 Princes Street | (*) tel. 0845 225 5121; Airport Tourist Information Desk | Airport | (*) tel. 0870 040 00 07

EDINBURGH PASS

You can purchase the Edinburgh Pass at the *Tourist Information Centre* at the airport, in the city centre *(3 Princes Street)* or, in advance, on the Internet *(www.edinburghpass.com)*. It consists of a 100-page booklet with a map of the city, bus plan, discount offers for many attractions, cafés and restaurants, a personalised pass and a bus ticket where you have to scratch out the date. With this pass, you are well-armed for one (£24), two (£36) or three days (£48). Children between 5 and 15 years of age, accompanied by an adult, pay £16, £24 and £32 respectively.

ELECTRICITY

230–240 volt alternating current. If you need it, you can buy an adapter for a three-pin plug in Edinburgh or ask at your hotel for one.

EMBASSIES & CONSULATES

CONSULATE OF THE UNITED STATES OF AMERICA
3 Regent Terrace, Edinburgh, EH7 5BW | tel. (44) 131 556 8315 | http://edinburgh. usconsulate.gov

AUSTRALIAN HONORARY CONSULATE
Mitchell House, 5 Mitchell Street, Edinburgh, EH6 7DB | tel. (44) 131 538 0582 | www.dfat.gov.au/missions/countries/ uked.html

CONSULATE OF CANADA
Burness, 50 Lothian Road, Edinburgh, EH3 9WJ | tel. (44) 131 473 6320 | www.canada international.gc.ca/united_kingdom

CONSULATE GENERAL OF IRELAND
16 Randolph Crescent | Edinburgh EH3 7TT | tel: (44) 131 226 7711 | www.irishconsulate scotland.co.uk

EMERGENCY SERVICES

Police, fire brigade, emergency doctor: tel. 999

HEALTH

For non-UK residents, the European Insurance card issued by your social security office is accepted in hospitals run by the *National Health Service (NHS)* and most doctors. In special cases, you will have to pay directly and submit your bill for refunding when you return home. Information in Edinburgh

INTERNET & WIFI

Visit Britain now gives advice exclusively via the Internet. The Edinburgh website *www.edinburgh.org* is especially recommendable. Accommodation can also be booked there (as well as at: *www.guide. visitscotland.com*). Other informative sites are: *www.edinburgh.com* and *www.edin burghguide.com*. Information on events can be found in the online editions of the daily newspapers The Scotsman *(www. thescotsman.scotsman.com)*, the event calendar The List *(www.list.co.uk)*, the national portal *www.ticketmaster.co.uk* (enter Edinburgh in the search field), from *www.eventsedinburgh.co.uk* and *www. edinburghfestivals.co.uk*. Information on live concerts under: *www.gigguide.co.uk*. Interesting facts on the architecture of the Scottish metropolis are listed under *www. edinburgharchitecture.co.uk*, Edinburgh's literary circles get together at *www.edin burghwriters.com*. Weather forecasts: *uk.weather.com*

Edinburgh now has a very good network. If you bring your laptop or Internet mobile phone with you, you will be able to surf on the Internet using WiFi in most hotels and an increasing number of bed & breakfasts – usually, free of charge. Many hotels have computer facilities in the lobby or a business centre where you can check your mails and get information. If you do not want to take advantage of these services, there are several Internet cafés in the city including: *Edinburgh Internet Café (daily 10am–11pm | 98 West Bow | Old Town); Easyinternetcafé (daily 7.30am–10.30pm | 58 Rose Street | New Town)*.

LEFT LUGGAGE

At the airport, the main Waverly Station and the bus station on St Andrew Square.

NEWSPAPERS & MAGAZINES

The leading newspaper in the capital is *The Scotsman (www.thescotsman.scotsman. com)*. Major international newspapers are also available but not always on the day of publication. The excellent event

THE RULES OF THE GAME

Football has a much harder time in Edinburgh than in Glasgow: the two more than 130-year-old local clubs *Heart of Midlothian* and *Hibernian* – the Hearts and Hibs for short – just do not whip up the enthusiasm of Celtic and the Rangers to the west. As is the case in Glasgow, the following has something to do with religion: the Hibs are Catholic like Celtic and the Hearts and Rangers are both Protestant. Tickets for the games of the two capital-city clubs start at £24; fans should book in advance via the Internet under *www. euroteam.net*. This is also the site where you can book tickets for the games of the Scottish National Rugby Team; a sport that is firmly anchored in the belligerent soul of the Scottish people. The Scottish team's home games are played in spring during the Six Nations Championship – a kind of Rugby Union European Championship. It is much easier however to get tickets for the games of the Edinburgh Rugby Team *(www.scottishrugby.org)*.

calendar *The List (www.list.co.uk)* is published every second Thursday. Fans of pop music will like *Is this Music (www.isthismusic.com)*. The quarterly *Chapman (www.chapman-pub.co.uk)* gives information on all the current news in the literary scene.

PERSONAL SAFETY

Edinburgh is a fairly safe city, at night as well as during the day. The typical entertainment areas around Cowgate and Tollcross are always very lively at weekends and you should count on meeting a few exuberant drunks.

PHONES & MOBILE PHONES

The dialling code for Edinburgh is 0131. For calls from abroad, dial 0044 (Great Britain) 131. Mobile numbers begin with 077, 078 or 079. 0800 and 0808 numbers are toll-free; premium rate numbers start with 09. Many telephone boxes operate with a credit card and shops with the BT symbol, such as chemist's, post offices and newsagents, sell phone cards. Check with you mobile-phone provider to find out which is the most economical roaming partner. If you use a Scottish prepaid card, you will not be charged for incoming calls. Texting is still the least expensive means of communication. If travelling from outside the UK, turn your mobile mailbox off before you leave home as this can cause high costs when you are abroad.

POST

Post offices are open from *9am to 5.30pm, Mon–Fri* and from *9am to noon on Sat*. You can purchase single stamps from post offices *(40 Frederick Street | New Town;*

WEATHER IN EDINBURGH

	Jan	Feb	March	April	May	June	July	Aug	Sept	Oct	Nov	Dec
Daytime temperatures in °C/°F												
	5/41	6/43	8/46	11/52	14/57	17/63	18/64	18/64	16/61	12/54	9/48	7/45
Nighttime temperatures in °C/°F												
	1/34	1/34	2/36	4/39	6/43	9/48	11/52	11/52	9/48	7/45	4/39	2/36
Sunshine hours/day												
	2	3	2	5	6	6	5	5	4	3	2	2
Precipitation days/month												
	17	15	15	14	14	15	17	16	16	17	17	18

46 St Mary's Street | Old Town) and booklets with several stamps in shops with the Royal Mail sign. Postcards require a 60p stamp.

PUBLIC TRANSPORT

There is an excellent network of buses *(www.lothianbuses.com)*. A single ticket costs £1.30, a day ticket £3. However, the city is small and the distances within the Old Town, New Town, Dean Village and Stockbridge are perfect for walking. Edinburgh reintroduced trams in 2011; they connect the airport with Leith and travel down Princes Street. The differences in altitude in the north-south direction make a comprehensive tram network impossible.

TIME

Greenwich Mean Time; daylight saving time starts and finishes on the same dates as in continental Europe. The North American east coast is 5 hours behind, the west coast 8 hours.

TIPPING

It is usual to tip taxi drivers and in restaurants. Round the bill up by about 10 percent. If the restaurant bill or menu states service charge included, this means that the tip has already been taken into account and it is not necessary to give anything extra. Tipping is not usual in pubs.

WEATHER

The Scots used to call Edinburgh 'Auld Reekie' – old smokie. Until 50 years ago, thick smoke poured out of the countless chimneys of the high-rise buildings that were still heated with coal. Today, Edinburgh is almost like a climatic health resort

A much-loved piece of British history

with often dramatic, cloud-framed views of the North Sea that you can admire from the hills. Sometimes fog – called *haar* – makes its way into the city from April to September; this is caused by warm air condensing over the cold North Sea. Winter is a good time to visit Edinburgh when, on clear days, the low-lying sun creates a dramatic play of light on the Old Town.

WEIGHTS & MEASURES

For overseas visitors: officially, Edinburgh (and all of Great Britain) calculates with the metric and decimal systems but the imperial standards are still used in everyday life: 1 inch = 2.54 cm; 1 foot = 30.48 cm; 1 yard = 91.44 cm; 1 mile = 1.609 km; 1 ounce = 28.35 g; 1 pound = 453.59 g; 1 pint = 0.5683 l; 1 gallon = 4.5459 l.

NOTES

MARCO POLO TRAVEL GUIDES

STREET ATLAS

The green line ▬▬ indicates the Walking tours (p. 82–87)

All tours are also marked on the pull-out map

Photo: Edinburgh Castle

Exploring Edinburgh

The map on the back cover shows how the area has been sub-divided

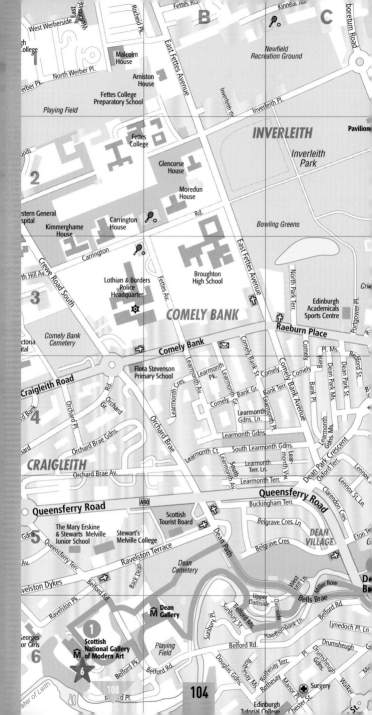

West Werberside

B

C

boretum Road

East Werberside

Rochcid Pk.

Fettes Ro.

Kinnear Ro.

West Werberside

1

College

Malcolm
House

North Werber Pl.

Arniston
House

erber Pk.

Fettes College
Preparatory School

Playing Field

Newfield
Recreation Ground

East Fettes Avenue

Inverleith Gr.

Inverleith Pl.

Inverleith Pl.

INVERLEITH

Pavilion

oods

Fettes
College

Inverleith
Park

2

Glencorse
House

Moredun
House

stern General
spital

Kimmerghame
House

Carrington
House

Carrington

Rd.

East Fettes Avenue

Bowling Greens

th Hill Av.

Crewe Road South

Carrington

Lothian & Borders
Police
Headquarter

Fettes Av.

Broughton
High School

North Park Terr.

Edinburgh
Academicals
Sports Centre

Cri

Portgower Pl.

3

COMELY BANK

Raeburn Place

ctoria
ital

Comely Bank
Cemetery

Comely Bank

Pl. Ms.

Belford St.

Comely

Dean Park St.

Comely

Bank

Comely Bank St.

Comely Bank Gr.

Bank Terr.

Comely Bank Ms.

Dean Park Ms.

Dean Pl.

B

Craigleith Road

Rd.

Flora Stevenson
Primary School

Learmonth Cres.

Learmonth Pk.

Learmonth Av.

Comely Gr.

Comely Bank Pl.

Learmonth
Gdns. Ln.

Learmonth Gdns. Ms.

Dean Park Crescent

Oxford Terr.

Lennox St.

4

Orchard
Gr.

Orchard Pl.

Orchard Brae Gdns.

Orchard Brae

Learmonth Ct.

Learmonth Gdns.

South Learmonth Gdns.

Lennox St. Ln.

d Rd.

ard

CRAIGLEITH

Orchard Brae Av.

South
Learmonth Av.

Learmonth
Terr. Ln.

Learmonth
Terr. Vw.

Learmonth Terr.

Clarendon Cres.

Lennox

Queensferry Road

A90

Buckingham Terr.

**DEAN
VILLAGE**

Eton Te

G

5

Gdns

The Mary Erskine
& Stewarts Melville
Junior School

Stewart's
Melville College

Scottish
Tourist Board

Belgrave Cres. Ln.

Queensferry Road

Queensferry Terr.

Ravelston Terrace

Dean Path

Belgrave Cres.

Av.

velston Dykes

Belford Rd.

Back Dean

Dean
Cemetery

Upper
Damside

West
Mill Ln.

Miller Row

Bells Brae

De
B

avelston Dykes

Ravelston Pk.

Sunbury Pl.

Sunbury St.

Belford Mk.

Damside

Haughhorbank Ln.

Belford Rd.

Lynedoch Pl. Ln.

Georges
or Girls

1

**Ⓜ Dean
Gallery**

Playing
Field

Belford Rd.

Drumsheugh
Gdns.

**Ⓜ Scottish
National Gallery
of Modern Art**

Belford Pk.

Belford Rd.

Sunbury
Pl.

Douglas Gdns.

Rothesay Terr.

Rothesay Ms.

Rothesay Pl.

Manor Pl.

Drumsheugh
Gdns.

Walker

Me

6

★

6

ater of Leith

108

104

d Pl.

Edinburgh
Tutorial College

Chester St.

St.

Surgery

Ravelston

Belgrave Cres.

Edinburgh
College of Art

E

Inverleith Pl.

Inverleith Pl. Ln.

Health
Centre

Inverleith Row

Warriston Dr.

Eildon Terr.

F

WARRISTON

Warriston
Cemetery

1

Warriston Av.

0   300 yd

200 m

Eildon St.

Recreation
Ground

Business
Park

Inverleith
House

Royal Botanic
Garden & Arboretum

Herbarium

Warriston Cres.

Logie Green Rd.

Logie
Green
Gdns.

Inverleith Row

Warriston Rd.

Boat Gn.

Catherine

CANONMILLS

2

Rock
Garden

Inverleith Terr.

Inverleith Terr. Ln.

Canon-
mills

Rodney Stre

Brou

Inverleith Terr.

Water of Leith

Brandon
Terr.

Canon St.

Eye Cres.

Glenogle Rd.

Liddes-
dale Pl.

Ettrick-
dale Pl.

Brandon St.

Logie

Canonmills
Special School

Corn

land St

H. Miller Pl.
Reid Terr.
Rintoul Pl.
Collins Pl.
Colville Pl.
Dunrobin Pl.
Balmoral Pl.

Kemp Pl.
Avondale Pl.
Teviotdale Pl.

Bell Pl.

Perth St.

Airlie Pl.

Eye Place

Eye Terr.

King George V
Playing Field

3

St. Bernard's Row

Saxe
Coburg Pl.

Saxe Coburg St.

The Edinburgh
Academy

Henderson Row

Henderson St.

Dundas St.

Royal

W. Scot-
land St. Ln.

Scotland St.

Cre

Avenue

Malta
Terr.

Deanhaugh St.

Hamilton Place

West Silvermills Ln.

Clarence St.

East Silvermills Ln.

Henderson
Pl. Ln.

Fettes Row

N.E. Cumberland St. Ln.

E. Cumberland St.

Drummond P

**NORTH
NEW T**

Place

1

STOCKBRIDGE

Leslie
Pl.

Veitch's
Sq.

Dean Bank Ln.

St. Stephen
St.

St. Stephen
St.

Fettes Row

N.W. Cumberland St. Ln.

Cumberland St.

S.W. Cumberland St. Ln.

Dundas St.

Great King St.

S.E. Cumberland St. Ln.

Northumberland St.
North East Ln.

Donaldson St.

Drummo

4

Theatre
Workshop

Carlton
St.

Saunders St.

Upper Dean St. Terr.

he St.

North West
Circus Pl.

Royal Circus

North East
Circus Pl.

South East
Circus Pl.

Alva Business
Centre

Great King St.

Northumberland St.
North West Ln.

Northumberland St.

Mackenzie
Pl.

India Pl.

Doune Terr.

Circus
Gdns.

Royal Circus

Jamaica St. North

Jamaica
St. North Ln.

Northumberland St.
South West Ln.

Northumberland St.
South East Ln.

Abercromby P

**St. Bernard's
Well**

Gloucester Ln.

India St.

Jamaica St.
South

Heriot Row

Queen

Dundas St.

**Scottish
Portra**

**Moray
Place
ardens**

Ainslie
Pl.

Great
Stuart St.

Moray Pl.

Darna-
way St.

Heriot Row

Street

Queen Stre

BBC Scotland

ph Crescent
ral
tre

Forres St.

St. Colme Street

Queen Street

North
Charlotte St.

Gardens

Thistle St.

Thistle St. N. E. Ln.

Thistle St.

Thistle St.

Thistle St. S. W. Ln.

Thistle St.

St. Andrew's

8

★

The D

Rose
Nort

Georgian
House

Glenfinlas
St.

Young St. North Ln.

Young St.

Young St. South Ln.

Hill St. North Ln.

Hill St.

Hill St. South Ln.

Belgrave
Business Centre

George

Frederick St.

Rose St. North Ln.

Rose St.

Rose St.

Hanover St.

Rose St.

Rose St.

Rose St.

Princes

**West Register
House**

Charlotte Sq.

Charlotte Sq.

Albert
Memorial

No 28

George

The Eye
Clinic

Castle St.

Castle St.

Assembly Rooms

Frederick St.

Rose St. South Ln.

**Royal Scottish
Academy**

Ea
Str

ph
ral
tre

Queensferry
St.

Randolph Cliff

Charlotte St.

Charlotte Sq.

Hope St.

Hope St. Ln.

Rose St. North Ln.

Rose St.

Rose St. South Ln.

Princes Street

Ross
Open Air
Theatre

Street Gardens

The Mound

**Nationa
Royal
Acade**

Write

Alva St.

Queensferry St. Ln.

St. John's
Church

105

Princes

109

Mound
Pl.

Glade

ace

St.

St. Cuthbert's
Church

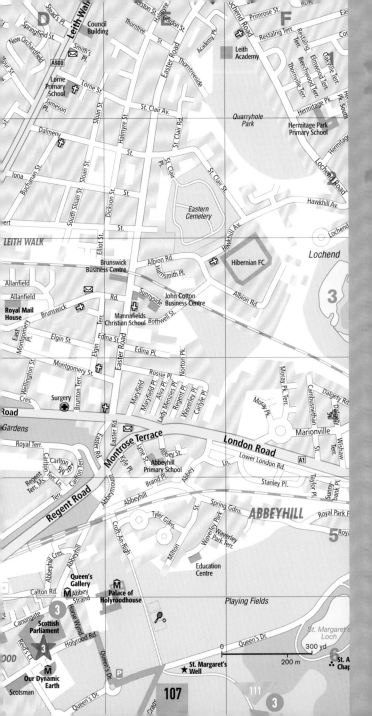

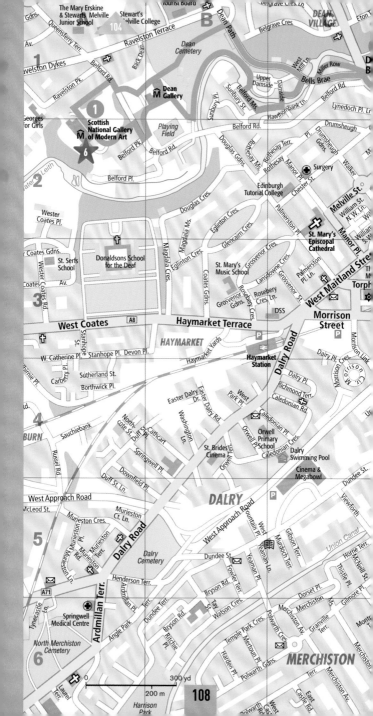

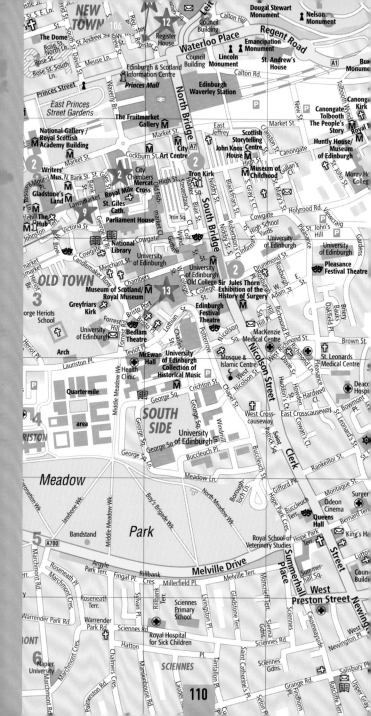

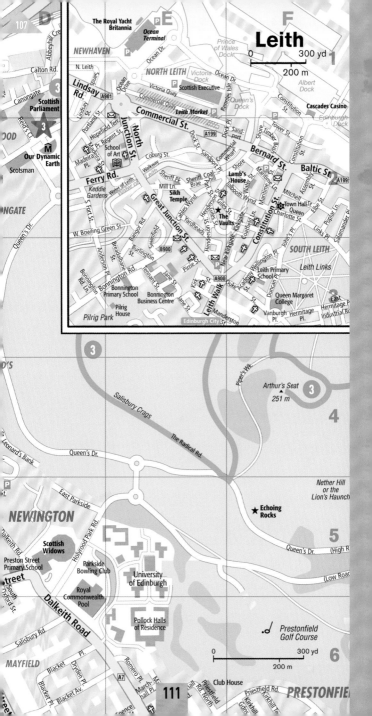

Leith

D **E** **F**

The Royal Yacht
Britannia

Ocean
Terminal

Prince
of Wales
Dock

NEWHAVEN

N. Leith

NORTH LEITH

Ocean Dr.

Ocean Dr.

Victoria
Dock

Albert
Dock

1

0   300 yd

200 m

Calton Rd.

Canongate

Lindsay
Rd.

A901

Scottish Executive

Ocean Dr

Queen's
Dock

Constitution St.

Cascades Casino

Edinburgh
Dock

Scottish
Parliament

Victoria Quay

Scottish Executive

Commercial Quay

Commercial St.

Leith Market

A199

Dock St.

Commercial
Wharf

Sand-
port

Shore

Tower St.

Timber Bush

Constitution St.

3

Our Dynamic
Earth

Scotsman

Hopefield Terr.

Pr. Regent St.

School
of Art

North Junction St.

Coburg St.

Bernard St.

Baltic St.

Maritime Ln.

A199

2

NGATE

Ferry Rd.

Keddie
Gardens

Madeira
Pl.

Fort St.

Water of Leith

Sheriff Bk.

Sheriff Brae

Mill Ln.

Sikh
Temple

Coal
Hill

Henderson St.

Tolbooth Wynd

Lamb's
House

Water St.

Giles St.

Maritime St.

Mitchell

Town Hall St.

Queen
Charlotte St.

Assembly St.

Poplar Ln.

Queen's Dr.

W. Bowling Green St.

Anderson Rd.

Great Junction St.

Burlington
St.

Swanfield

Yardheads

JS Anderson

St Giles St.

The
Vaults

Cadiz St.

Constitution St.

St. John's Pl.

SOUTH LEITH

Links Pl.

Salamander St.

3

Bonnington
Rd. Ln.

Breadalbane St.

Tennant St.

B900

Pirrie St.

Wellington Pl.

Leith Links

Bonnington Rd.

Jane St.

Kirk St.

A900

Duke St.

Academy St.

Queen Margaret
College

East
Hermitage Pl.

East
Hermitage Pk.
Industrial Rd.

Pilrig Park

Bonnington
Primary School

Pilrig
House

Bonnington
Business Centre

Jane St.

Leith Walk

Manderston St.

Duncan Pl.

Vanburgh
Pl.

Hermitage
Pl.

Edinburgh City St.

Leith Primary
School

Leith Primary
School Pl.

Bonnington
Primary School

3

Salisbury Craigs

Piper's Wk.

Arthur's Seat
251 m

3

4

Leonard's Bank

Queen's Dr.

The Radical Rd.

Nether Hill
or the
Lion's Haunch

NEWINGTON

East Parkside

Holyrood Park Rd.

★ Echoing
Rocks

Queen's Dr.

(High R

5

Scottish
Widows

Preston Street
Primary School

Dalkeith Rd

Parkside
Bowling Club

University
of Edinburgh

(Low Road

treet

South
Oxford St.

Royal
Commonwealth
Pool

Dalkeith Road

Salisbury Rd.

Pollock Halls
of Residence

Prestonfield
Golf Course

MAYFIELD

Blacket
Pl.

Dryden Pl.

Blacket Av.

A7

Romero Pl.

March-
hall Pl.

0   300 yd

200 m

6

Club House

Priestfield Rd.

Priestfield Rd. North

Kimball
Gdns.

Kirkhill Te

Priestfield Rd

Kirkhill Rd

PRESTONFIE

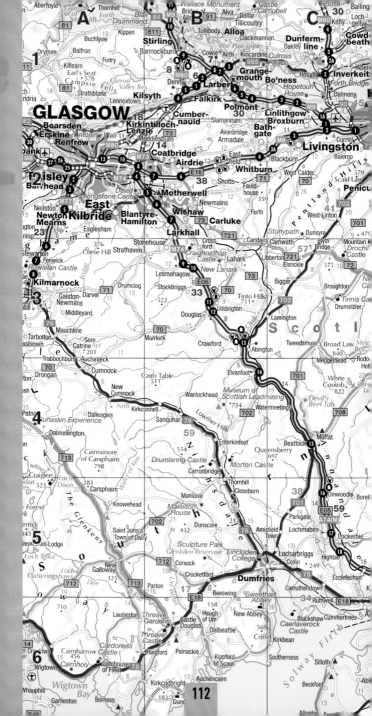

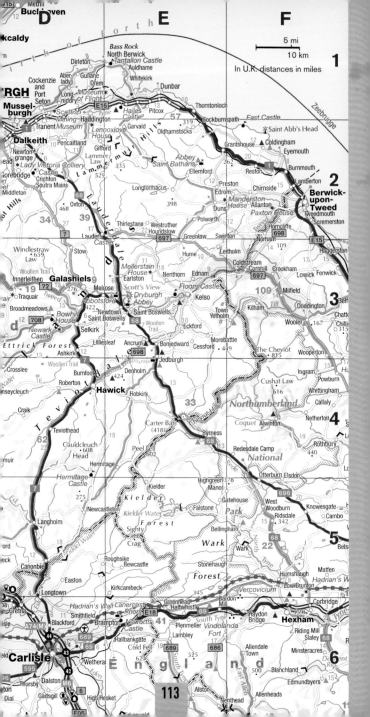

KEY TO STREET ATLAS

M̂	Museum
🎭	Stage / Bühne
ℹ	Information
✝	Church / Kirche
✡	Synagogue / Synagoge
☪	Mosque / Moschee
⊕	Hospital / Krankenhaus
✿	Police / Polizei
✉	Post
📖	Library / Bibliothek
♟	Monument / Denkmal
🚎	Bus terminal / Busbahnhof
∴	Ruin / Ruine
🎾	Tennis court / Tennisplatz
⛳	Golf course / Golfplatz
⌂	Indoor swimming pool / Hallenbad
P	Parking / Parkplatz
⚠	Youth Hostel / Jugendherberge
▭	Railway with station / Eisenbahn mit Bahnhof
▪	Remarkable building / Bemerkenswertes Gebäude
▪	Public building / Öffentliches Gebäude
▫	Green / Grünfläche
▫	Uncovered area / Unbebaute Fläche
▨	Pedestrian zone / Fußgängerzone
▬	Walking tours / Stadtspaziergänge
★1	MARCO POLO Highlight

INDEX

This index lists all places and sights, plus the names of important people featured in this guide. Numbers in bold indicate a main entry.

CREDITS

WRITE TO US

e-mail: info@marcopologuides.co.uk

Did you have a great holiday? Is there something on your mind? Whatever it is, let us know! Whether you want to praise, alert us to errors or give us a personal tip – MARCO POLO would be pleased to hear from you. We do everything we can to provide the very latest information for your trip.

Nevertheless, despite all of our authors' thorough research, errors can creep in. MARCO POLO does not accept any liability for this. Please contact us by e-mail or post.

MARCO POLO Travel Publishing Ltd Pinewood, Chineham Business Park Crockford Lane, Chineham Basingstoke, Hampshire RG24 8AL United Kingdom

PICTURE CREDITS
Cover photograph: The Royal Mile, military parade (mauritius images: Vidier)
Castle Inns (Stirling) Ltd. (16 bottom); Godiva (17 bottom); Rob Hoon (16 top); Huber: Mackie (102/103); © iStockphoto.com: Chris Price (17 top); M. Kirchgessner (60, 65, 88, 90, 90/91, 93); H. Krinitz (2 top, 4, 12/13, 30, 32, 34, 38/39, 44, 85, 99); Laif: Artz (22), Krinitz (43); mauritius images: Alamy (front flap right, 2 centre top, 3 bottom, 5, 6, 7, 15, 24 left, 40, 56 right, 74/75, 78, 92 top, 117), Vidier (1 top, 20); M. Müller (1 bottom); T. Stankiewicz (front flap left, 2 centre bottom, 2 bottom, 3 top, 3 centre, 7, 8, 9, 10/11, 18/19, 24 right, 25, 26/27, 36, 46, 49, 50/51, 52, 55, 56 left, 57, 58/59, 63, 66/67, 68, 70/71, 73, 76, 80, 82/83, 86, 88/89, 89, 92 bottom); Ian J. Watson (16 centre)

1st Edition 2012
Worldwide Distribution: Marco Polo Travel Publishing Ltd, Pinewood, Chineham Business Park, Crockford Lane, Basingstoke, Hampshire RG24 8AL, United Kingdom. Email: sales@marcopolouk.com
© MAIRDUMONT GmbH & Co. KG, Ostfildern
Chief editors: Michaela Lienemann (concept, managing editor), Marion Zorn (concept, text editor)
Author: Martin Müller; editor: Jens Bey
Programme supervision: Ann-Katrin Kutzner, Nikolai Michaelis, Silwen Randebrock
Picture editor: Gabriele Forst
What's hot: wunder media, Munich
Cartography street atlas and pull-out map: DuMont Reisekartografie, Fürstenfeldbruck; © MAIRDUMONT, Ostfildern
Design: milchhof : atelier, Berlin; Front cover, pull-out map cover, page 1: factor product munich
Translated from German by Robert McInnes; editor of the English edition: Christopher Wynne

DOS & DON'TS 👆

How to not rub people up the wrong way in Edinburgh

DON'T WAIT FOR YOUR BEER IN A PUB

In a pub, you have to order your drinks and food at the bar and pay for them at the same time. The food is then brought to your table.

WAIT UNTIL THE LIGHT TURNS GREEN

Pedestrians have to press a button at a traffic light if they want it to turn green. However, the locals are frequently cross when it is red if there is no traffic.

ONLY PAY FOR YOUR OWN DRINK

If you go on a pub crawl with a group of locals, there are always as many rounds as there are participants. The drinks are paid for in turn. So, make sure the group is small if you don't want to end up under the table.

DON'T CALL THE SCOTS ENGLISH

You are actually in Great Britain or the United Kingdom but definitely not in England. Don't forget to call the people *Scottish* even if *English* is on the tip of your tongue. By the way: Scotch is also incorrect: that's the drink.

DON'T ORDER SCOTCH ON THE ROCKS

Of course you will be served whisky with ice if you ask for it. But, there is always a jug of water on the bar in the Whisky Capital so that you can put a few drops in your drink if you want to. As a rule, the Scots think that ice ruins the subtle taste of the 'water of life'.

SHAKING HANDS

For non-Brits: if you look closely, you will notice that shaking hands is not very common in Scotland – especially with women. You introduce yourself with your full name and then often continue on a first-name basis.

DON'T DRIVE YOUR OWN CAR

Don't cause yourself more stress than necessary; driving in the Old Town is often tricky business. If you don't feel like walking, catch a bus. That is what most of the locals do. You can buy tickets from the machines at the bus stops.

DON'T RAVE ABOUT GLASGOW

Don't let on that you think Glasgow is great. The two cities are completely different and there is no love lost between their inhabitants.

DON'T TRAVEL ON RUGBY WEEKENDS

Avoid visiting Edinburgh when Scotland is playing against other nations in the sold-out Murrayfield Stadium – especially during the Six Nations European Championship between February and April.